WHAT CAN I DO FOR
AN ART LESSON?

WHAT CAN I DO FOR AN ART LESSON?

by Ruth L. Peck

PARKER PUBLISHING COMPANY, INC.

A Practical Guide for the Elementary Classroom Teacher

and Robert S. Aniello

West Nyack, New York

What Can I Do for an Art Lesson? A Practical Guide for the Elementary Classroom Teacher, by Ruth L. Peck and Robert S. Aniello

LIBRARY OF CONGRESS
CATALOG CARD NUMBERS 66-12751

Fifth Printing..... January, 1968

PRINTED IN THE UNITED STATES OF AMERCIA

95197—B&P

To the Teacher

LIKE MOST ELEMENTARY TEACHERS, YOU MAY HAVE COMPLAINED that, "I can't teach art." Or perhaps you have asked, "What can I do for an art lesson?" These and similar comments may be the result of poor teaching by someone else when you yourself were a child. Or it may be just that as a present day elementary school teacher you feel the pressure of pulls from every direction and so you lack the time to think and to plan activities for the creative art growth of the children in your class.

But from whatever cause it may stem, you probably feel the need for guidance and suggestions for art activities that are worthwhile. It is for you—for all elementary school teachers—that this book has been written. It has been written to give you confidence that you are teaching art lessons that have value; it has been written for you in order that you may avoid searching for ideas in widely scattered places and so that you may thereby save time; it has been written for you so that you will enjoy teaching art and therefore will make it a pleasurable and valuable experience for children in your classes.

The authors are both art teachers in elementary schools and they understand your problems and the possibilities you have for teaching art under ordinary classroom conditions. They have therefore presented only those projects which have been successfully completed under situations likely to be found in most places—not just the ideal. Materials needed for the various lessons are those generally available as art supplies or which you can obtain easily.

Much has been said and written about art in the elementary school and you know that much of it is poles apart in its philosophy. It ranges from the stereotyped, follow-directions type which results in all look-alikes to the idea that all children are creative artists who need

v

only to be left alone with materials. We believe that neither of these views is either modern or realistic in its approach. Nothing will be gained by the children in your class when all the art learning has been by you, the teacher, and all that is left for the child is to manipulate materials in a specified way as you direct. Equally cheated is the child if you say, "He did it all by himself. I had nothing to do with it." Surely you have something to contribute to his knowledge. Unless you make that contribution, his learning will be the poorer for it.

Good art teaching is good *teaching*—not teacher dominated but teacher guided. The teacher who guides will realize that there is a relationship between a child's physical and mental growth and that all art materials and techniques are not equally appropriate to children of all ages. For this reason we have suggested a range of grade levels for each lesson described.

This book presents ideas and activities that involve general learning or understanding for all children. Therefore, an art lesson may be presented to a class as a whole, but in the application of that learning, individual creative art will result. Perhaps you are surprised not to find children's work as illustrations. Don't be—for how could one illustration show you all the many possibilities for that lesson! Instead be surprised by the infinite variety of interpretations which your children will have. Art should be as varied and as personal as the individual who creates it.

The practical, easy to follow lessons are in accord with the best of modern art education, yet they are presented on a pleasant person to person basis. Included are ways to adapt lessons so that you may use them at different grade levels, or you may vary the same lesson so that new but basic concepts will be retained by the child.

We recognize today that creative art expression has value to every child. But how to select and plan activities that will result in that individual, creative expression is undoubtedly a very real problem to you. This book will help you with that need by putting into your hands in one volume a series of art lessons that have meaning in a regular elementary school classroom. It is our hope that this book will also give you confidence in yourself and confidence in the art ability of your class. We hope that it will be a practical guide for you so that your art lessons will have purpose—and above all, we hope that you and your class will find art an increasingly pleasant teaching and learning experience.

RUTH L. PECK
ROBERT S. ANIELLO

Contents

CONTENTS

WHAT CAN I DO FOR AN ART LESSON?

PRIMARY GRADES

1.

Tempera Paint

CHAPTER **1**   *Tempera Paint*

Lesson One: Stand Up and Paint!

PAINTING PICTURES IN PRIMARY GRADES

ENJOY PAINTING WITH YOUR PRIMARY CLASS. THERE is nothing young children like to do more than to paint. Once they have done it several times, all they will need is to see the paints and brushes and they will be eager to go to work. It is the most basic of all primary grade art and should be repeated frequently.

So—let's paint today! If the children have painted often, all that will be necessary is to say, "Do you know what you would like to paint today?" But if this is the first time, or

4

is a relatively unfamiliar experience for them, you will have to take time to motivate it. Begin with a question such as, "What do you like to do more than anything else? What do you have the most fun doing?" Perhaps someone will suggest roller skating, or playing with a toy truck, or pretending to be a nurse. Get many ideas. Encourage each child to think for himself and say what he thinks would be more fun than anything else.

Then back up a bit. Choose one of the suggestions and begin to ask some questions about it. "What color is your toy truck?" "Would you rather play with it by yourself, or is it more fun to play with it when you have a friend with you?" Or, "You like to go roller skating. You would have to be outdoors for that, wouldn't you?" "Would it be in the summer? What kind of clothes would you have on?" "What would you see while you were roller skating?" As different children offer answers to the questions, get them to think of details—color, sound, feel, anything that makes the ideas more real.

When the discussion has reached a peak of interest and everyone has his own idea, arrange them into groups, distribute materials, stand up, and *paint!*

At first, concentrate only on the idea. Encourage each child to "say" what he likes with paint. Once this has been accomplished—and children will be eager to express their own ideas if they are sure that is what you really want and that you will approve—then you will be able to stress other things which will make their paintings more successful.

Encourage children to hold their brushes at or near the top of the handle. Many of them will do this from the beginning, but those children who are more timid about painting may hold it near the brush end—as one would hold a pencil. Stress that they paint with a brush—not a pencil—and that they hold a brush differently. This is important, because paint is a fluid material and should be applied with free, flowing motions. Also, holding the brush at the top encourages children to paint big, and thereby avoid tiny, fussy little pictures.

Holding the brush properly and applying the paint freely tends to make the picture big, and bigness should be encouraged—not as an end in itself, but as a means of rapid and free expression of an idea. To further encourage making things big, begin by talking about what is the most important part of the picture. If the boy is playing with his truck, *he* is more important than the truck. The girl who is roller skating is more important than the tree in the yard. Make the most important thing first—and make it the biggest. Grass, sky, and water are not as important and can be added at the very end, if at all.

Get children to fill their papers. Once the most important and biggest thing has been painted they should use the rest of the paper to add anything that is a part of what they are "telling" with paint. They will easily understand the difference between *filling* the paper and *crowding* it. Perhaps you can use their own classroom as an example to help them understand this. Point out that even though there are 20 or 30 children in the room, there are still some spaces in the front and back of the room and in the aisles. "But what would happen if everyone in the class across the hall came in here, too? They would be able to get in, wouldn't they? But it would be ———" and some-one will almost automatically end the sentence by saying "crowded." Fill the picture but don't crowd it.

But most important of all is to paint, paint, paint—and then paint some more. The more you do it the easier it gets—for the children and for you.

Make It Easy—for Yourself!

1. Organize children into groups of from three to six. In a regular classroom, four desks can be pushed together to make a group. Place painting materials on one desk and have three children at the others, one at each desk. Or use any similar arrangement that leaves one desk free for supplies.
2. Cover all work areas—including the desk for supplies—with newspaper.
3. Have small cans for water to wash brushes—one can for each group. Small cans the size frozen juice comes in are suitable, easy for small children to handle, and take little storage space.
4. Use egg cartons for distribution of paints. The regular pressed-type cartons can be broken in half to provide six compartments for six different colors. Even the youngest children then can carry all the paints at one time for one group. The half carton is stable and will not tip over. Children will be able to provide an ample supply of cartons.

5. Plastic detergent bottles make ideal paint dispensers. Paint in them remains moist and ready to use from one lesson to another. They offer an easy way of filling egg cartons (or other paint containers) without spilling.

6. Assign one child from each group as the helper for the lesson. Have him (1) cover all desks (in his group) with newspaper, (2) give each child a piece of painting paper (easel paper—unprinted news, 18 x 24), (3) give each child an easel brush, (4) get a can of water for the group, and (5) get an egg carton of paint for the group.

7. No pencils! No drawing first—just paint.

8. Be sure children stand up to paint. It permits greater freedom of motion, insures fewer accidents, and results in better pictures.

9. Clean up the easy way. The helper collects brushes from his group and lays them on a paper towel or newspaper for washing later. Collect brushes first so as to avoid the possibility of continued painting once the picture has been finished. Have the helper empty the can of water in the sink (or a pail if there is no sink), and have the carton of used paint brought to you. Empty it into the sink (or pail). Pile the used cartons together and wrap them in a newspaper before discarding. Fold newspaper, collect, and throw away.

10. When not in use, always store brushes flat in a box or stand them on the wooden ends in a can.

Variations

1. Illustrate real stories: "Humpty Dumpty," "Millions of Cats."

2. Make up a simple story and tell to the class. Illustrate it.

3. Paint pictures of real people: My Teacher; My Mother; Myself.

4. Suggest a specific topic to be illustrated: A Cold Day; What I'll Be When I Grow Up; Helping My Father at Home.

5. Paint on colored paper.

6. Add real materials for a novelty touch: twigs, cloth, yarn.

OBJECTIVES

1. **To express a personal idea with an art material that makes a rapid expression possible.**

2. **To gain confidence in expressing an idea with a fluid material.**

3. **To translate an idea into visual form.**

4. **To learn about the action of paint on wet paper and how to use it to advantage.**

(For grades 2 and 3)

Lesson Two: We Can Be Lazy!

PAINTING ON WET PAPER

LET'S BE DIFFERENT WITH OUR PAINTING TODAY. We'll get the paper wet, and then we can be lazy while the water does most of the work for us. Begin as you would for any painting lesson—stimulate ideas: talk about what they're going to paint, what will be important in their pictures. Make their ideas real by having them talk about what the clown looked like, what he did. Or the sound the train made and what it looked like as it sped by. Or how big the fish was that he caught and what his father said about it.

Then tell them that they should only paint the biggest, most im-

8

portant parts of their "story" because they are going to paint on wet paper, and the water will make all the little things disappear. Perhaps show them what you mean.

Pour a puddle of water on a 12 x 18 manila drawing paper, then immediately spread it over the whole paper with the palm of your hand flat on the paper. At once begin painting something large, perhaps a tall tree. Notice how the water spreads the paint and carries it away from where you put it. But that's all right because today the water is going to help make my picture, and I can go over some of it again if I want to. Add some big branches—then some tiny ones that disappear. See, the water doesn't like little things painted on it. So let's go over just the bigger things. Enjoy the fuzzy edges that appear—make it important that the water is painting part of your picture.

Then everybody to work! Arrange the children into groups, distribute materials, stand up, and you and the water paint!

Encourage each child to paint big, to repaint areas that the water has nearly made disappear. Stop—look at what is happening to the picture—then decide what else you and the water need to do to finish your picture.

Remind the children to hold their brushes at the top of the handle. This, remember, encourages big motions and big pictures—especially needed when painting on wet paper.

Oh, of course, fill the paper! Let the water help with that, too. Perhaps just interesting colors, moved about and made fuzzy by the water, would make an interesting background for the picture.

Now that was fun, wasn't it? And wasn't it easy when something else did part of the painting for you? A little longer than usual to dry, a display of as many as possible—then just be ready to answer questions about how they were done.

Make It Easy—for Yourself!

1. Organize children into groups of three. Four desks may be pushed together to form a painting area for three children, the fourth desk to be used for supplies: paint, water, brushes.
2. Cover all work areas with newspaper.
3. Two small cans of water for each group will make get-

ting the paper wet and ready for painting move faster. The extra water may then be poured into one can for each group to use to wash brushes. The teacher can remove the extra can during the lesson to assist an easy clean-up.

4. Use egg cartons for distribution of paint. The regular, pressed type cartons broken in half provide space for six colors and are stable enough not to tip over.

5. Plastic detergent bottles make ideal paint dispensers. Use them to fill the egg cartons before the painting lesson begins.

6. Appoint one child from each group as a helper for that lesson. Have him (1) cover all desks in his group with newspaper, (2) give each child a piece of 12 x 18 manila drawing paper, (3) give each child an easel brush, (4) get two cans of water for the group, and (5) get an egg carton of paint for the group.

7. No pencils! No drawing first—just paint.

8. Stand up to paint. It permits greater freedom of motion, insures fewer accidents, and results in better pictures.

9. Clean up the easy way. The helper collects brushes from his group and leaves them on a newspaper for washing later. The helper then empties the can of water into the sink (or pail), and brings the carton of paint to you to be emptied into the sink (or pail). Pile the used cartons together and wrap them in a newspaper before discarding. Fold newspapers, collect, and throw away.

10. Store brushes flat in a box or stand them on the wooden ends in a can.

Variations

1. Illustrate real stories—those they have read or those that the teacher has told.

2. Paint just with colors (no attempt to make anything real).

3. Paint moods: The Way I Feel when I'm Happy; The Way I Feel when I'm Sad; The Way I Feel when I'm Excited.

Lesson Three: Time for a Change!

PRIMARY TO SECONDARY COLORS

It's time for a change! let's turn a primary grade painting class into an experimental laboratory. The class will become inventors delving into the mysteries of primary and secondary colors. It'll be a welcome change for you and for the class after having done a lot of realistic painting.

All you need are three colors (red, yellow, and blue), a small piece of paper for experiments (9 x 12 or 12 x 18), and a big 18 x 24 paper for your painting. Begin with a discussion about scientists and inventors. Talk about what they do and how they do it—that they don't always succeed the first time. Stress the fact that they have problems to solve—then end the discussion on the note that the class, too, has a problem to solve.

Each person's problem is to make a painting that has six colors, but only three colors can be used—red, yellow, and blue. How is that possible? Can you think of any way that it can be done? Well, let's see if you get a new color if you mix two of them together.

On a piece of paper paint an area of yellow, then add a little blue to it and mix them together. Sure enough, there's a beautiful green. So now we have four colors. All right, let's try yellow again but this time add red to it. See, a different color. This time we have orange— but we still need one more new color, purple. How do you think you could make that? That's right. We haven't mixed blue with red yet. But there it is now, a fine purple.

Explain that red, yellow, and blue are called *primary* colors because they are the most important colors and are used to make three other colors called *secondary* colors. Set them up on your paper in the form of an equation. Paint a band of yellow, next to it make a plus sign, then next to that paint a band of blue. Finally make an equal sign and paint a band of yellow and blue blended together to make green. In the same way make an equation for each of the other color combinations. Display the color equations in the room for easy reference.

Do you think that green always looks the same, like this green? What would have happened if I had put more yellow in it? That's right. It would have been a yellow green. Or more blue would have been a blue green.

Now, how about each of you becoming an inventor. See how many kinds of green you can make, and how many kinds of orange and purple you can make.

When enough experimenting has been done, give out the big pieces of paper so that each person can make a picture having at least six colors from the original three. (Some children may discover that by mixing all three primary colors together they will make brown or black.) Let them make either abstract or realistic pictures as long as they create a variety of color.

You'll find that the class will respond enthusiastically and, through doing, will learn much about color that they will continue to use. Remember that this is an experimental introduction to color, so more stress should be placed on the doing of color than on the theory of color. Then display the paintings (and perhaps some of the experiments, too) so that the learning experience becomes a successful experience for the child—for he will see that *you* value it, too.

Make It Easy—for Yourself!

1. Arrange children into groups of two or more depending upon conditions in the room.
2. Cover all work areas with newspaper.
3. Have a small can of water for each group.
4. Use papier mâché type of egg cartons broken in half for distribution of paint.
5. Use plastic detergent bottles as paint dispensers.
6. Appoint one helper from each group to (1) cover all desks in his group with newspaper, (2) give each person paper for experiments, (3) give each person a brush, (4) get a can of water for the group, and (5) get an egg carton of paint for the group.
7. No pencils! No drawing first—just paint.
8. Stand up to paint for greater freedom of motion, better pictures, and fewer accidents.
9. Clean up the easy way. Have the helper collect brushes from his group and leave them on a newspaper for washing later. Then have the helper empty the can of water into the sink (or pail), and bring the carton of paint to you to be emptied into the sink (or pail). Pile the used cartons together and wrap them in a newspaper before discarding. Fold newspapers, collect, and throw away.
10. Store brushes flat in a box or stand them on the wooden ends in a can.

Variation

Paint with other painting tools (sponges, swab sticks) using only the primary colors.

Variation for Lower Grades

In any painting experience use only the primary colors. Let the mixing to form new colors be more accidental than planned.

Variations for Higher Grades

1. Create a picture (abstract or realistic) by making as many color variations as possible from any two primary colors. For example: Make a picture using blue and yellow and as many varied combinations of the two as possible.
2. Paint swatches of color using any two primary colors. For example: Make a swatch of blue and red and then swatches of many varieties of red purple, purple, and blue purple. Use these swatches as you would regular colored paper to create a cut paper picture.

Lesson Four: Painting in Particular

PAINTING PICTURES IN INTERMEDIATE GRADES

ART IN GENERAL, AND PAINTING IN PARTICULAR, has become an integral part of American culture. Society is demanding more and more art for home and industry, and more and more people are delving into the arts as hobbies to fulfill their creative urge. To meet this demand it is important for young people to have a good foundation in art—and up to the teacher to supply it.

The backbone of all art is painting, but too many people feel that tempera painting is only for the primary grades. With a little help, the classroom teacher of the upper elementary grades can make tempera painting the exciting and valuable learning experience that it should be. Here is that help.

The biggest problem in painting faced by the upper grade teacher is how to get away from the flat appearing paintings of the lower grades which have now become a stereotype. Because of the thick consistency of tempera paint it is natural and right for young children to paint in broad, flat areas, but it is now time for the older child to become more aware of the world around him. He should notice that colors in nature are not flat and dull. The grass in a meadow does not look like wall-to-wall carpeting, and trees are not flat sticks with lollipops on top. The child should become aware of the many different shades found in one general color. He should see the yellows and blues in green fields and leaves; the light and dark of a troubled sky; the greens and blues and browns of the ocean; the vivid colors and delicate shadings of a sunset. Even man-made objects have lights and darks where light and shadow hit them. How can you show these gradations of color in a medium which naturally lends itself to flat tones? The answer is water.

Tempera is a water base paint and can be controlled by the amount of water used with it. Used as it comes from the jar it produces a flat tone. If it is diluted, it produces effects ranging from opaque to transparent, depending upon the amount of water used. In order to achieve a dark to light gradation on paper, paint is applied full strength, then thinned with water. Another way is to apply paint to different parts of a wet area and let the paint spread, resulting in dark to light tones. Paint dropped into wet paint produces still another gradation of tone and mixing of colors. This can all be demonstrated to the class, letting them see that tempera paint has a greater potential for pictures than they had thought. If time permits, let them experiment, too, or use this experimentation as a lesson in itself.

After you and the class have done some experimenting with tempera paint to achieve gradation of color, plan to use the increased understanding and skill by painting a picture. Use as large a paper as possible, preferably 18 x 24. Have the class look out the windows. Notice the different varieties of one color. See, nothing looks flat. Even the street has shadings of color in it.

Then ask each child to think of a scene with which he is familiar. Tell him to "think in technicolor," trying to remember as many color details as possible so that he can reproduce it for everyone to enjoy.

Have each child block out his scene, as a guide for himself, with slightly tinted water. Then as the painting begins, concentrate on as much color gradation as possible. Avoid using too much detail, but rather work in large areas. This will permit spaces big enough to really show variations in color. Emphasize the use of a *lot* of water and the mixing of colors.

The results will be more exciting than you expected and far different from the average child's painting. But more important, the awareness of color variations and the learning of new skills will be an excellent foundation for the future. It is a lesson which never can be repeated too often—and it will be enjoyed every time.

Make It Easy—for Yourself!

1. Arrange the children in groups of from two to four each. Two rows may be pushed together or four desks may be pushed together to form a painting area for three children, the fourth desk to be used for supplies.
2. Cover all work areas with newspaper.
3. Place a can of water on a desk in each group.
4. Use egg cartons for distribution of paint. A papier mâché carton broken in half provides space for six colors.
5. Plastic detergent bottles make ideal paint dispensers. Use them to fill the egg cartons before the painting class begins.
6. Appoint a helper from each group to give out materials to his group: newspapers on desks, 18 x 24 manila or white drawing paper, easel brushes (large watercolor brushes would be a help, too), can of water, carton of paint.
7. No pencils! Block out large areas with light tint of paint.
8. Stand up to paint for greater freedom of motion, resulting in better pictures and fewer accidents.
9. Clean up the easy way. Have the helper collect the brushes from his group and leave them on a newspaper for washing later. Then he should empty the can of water into the sink (or pail), bring the carton of paint to you to empty into the sink (or pail). Pile the used cartons together and wrap them in a newspaper before discarding them. Have the children fold their newspapers. Collect and throw them away.
10. Store brushes flat in a box or stand them on the wooden ends in a can.

Variations

1. Use the same techniques for still life arrangements, concentrating on color variations to create a 3-D effect.
2. Use these techniques for painting specific themes: clowns, seascapes, hurricane.
3. Create a completely abstract picture by mixing colors.

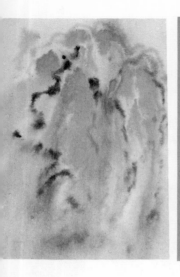

OBJECTIVES

1. **To introduce the idea that color is important in creating a mood or feeling.**

2. **To learn to mix paints as a means of increasing the potential of color.**

3. **To increase the understanding of color and how to combine colors for greater variety.**

4. **To learn how water acts as a mixing medium with a fluid material.**

(For grades 3 and 4, adapted to grades 5 and 6)

Lesson Five: Have You Ever Felt Blue?

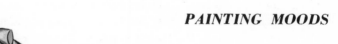

PAINTING MOODS

HAVE YOU EVER FELT BLUE? OR GREEN WITH ENVY? or purple with rage? or yellow with fear? or red with embarrassment? Have you ever felt the cool quietness of a room decorated in blues and greens—or the warmth and cheerfulness of a room done in reds and oranges? Colors have come to represent many moods and feelings, and this can be a wonderful idea for an art lesson which introduces the moods of color as well as an understanding of non-objective painting.

Discuss with the class the feelings that a color represents. Talk about how they could use a color to express a mood or feeling. What is a happy color? Sure, red is a very happy color. Also yellow and orange. What colors do you think are sad? Right! Blue and green are sad, especially if they are dark or dull.

How does nature use color to show what kind of mood she is in? Are colors bright and cheery during a rainstorm? Of course not. They become dull and heavy looking. What does the sky look like on a bright summer day? What kind of colors would you use to show a hurricane or a tornado?

When the class has become aware of the moods and attitudes that colors can represent, make a list on the chalk board of all moods they can think of. Give each child a piece of 12 x 18 white drawing paper. Have him wet it thoroughly. A little puddle of water can be poured on from a small can and then spread over the entire paper with the flat part of the hand as if fingerpainting.

Then, by just using color, create one of the moods which has beeen listed on the chalkboard. Make sure they understand that they are to make nothing real. Only the colors of the tempera paint are to tell the mood.

Because the colors will run on the wet paper they are difficult to control (but that is an important part of the technique). Therefore, let each child make at least two tries. When a successful mood painting has been achieved, have the child label it in pencil on the back of his picture.

Make sure of two things: that you have a wide variety of colors to choose from and that the paintings are done quickly and are not overworked. Working on a painting too long or brushing it too much will produce a blurred, muddy quality and destroy the intended mood. So stop—stop—*stop* before this happens.

After the class has cleaned up and the paintings are dry enough to hold up without the paint running, let the class try guessing the moods. Have each child choose one of his best pictures and hold it up for the others to guess what mood he painted.

These paintings make an effective display. Arrange them on a bulletin board and make a title for each of the moods. Use a caption such as "Match the Mood!" to tell your story and create interest.

Similarity between the children's work and abstract "modern" art should be pointed out. If prints of non-objective paintings are available they could be displayed about the room. The class—and you, too—will enjoy and learn much from them if you try to feel what mood they suggest, and how the artist has done it.

Make It Easy—for Yourself!

1. Organize children into groups of three. Four desks may

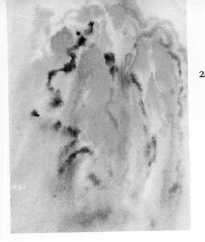

be pushed together to form a painting area for three children, the fourth desk to be used for supplies: paint, water, brushes. Four to six children may be in one group if large tables are available.

2. Cover all work areas with newspaper.

3. Have small cans of water to wash brushes in—one can for each group.

4. Use egg cartons for distribution of paints. They may be broken in half to provide space for six colors.

5. Use plastic detergent bottles as paint dispensers to fill egg cartons.

6. Assign one child from each group as a helper. Have him (1) cover all desks in his group with newspaper, (2) give each child a piece of 12 x 18 white drawing paper, (3) give each child an easel brush or large watercolor brush, (4) get a can of water for his group, and (5) get an egg carton of paint for his group.

7. Stand up to paint for greater freedom of motion, fewer accidents, and better results.

8. Clean up the easy way. Have the helper collect brushes from his group and leave them on a newspaper for washing later. Then have the helper empty the can of water into the sink (or pail), bring the carton of paint to you to be emptied into the sink (or pail). Pile the used cartons together and wrap them in a newspaper before discarding. Fold newspapers, collect, and throw away.

9. Store brushes flat in a box or stand them on the wooden ends in a can.

Variations

1. Work on 12 x 18 colored construction paper. Pick a color that will indicate the mood, wet the paper, then add paint to further bring out that mood.

2. Paint a realistic picture which depicts a mood: the approaching storm; a happy day; the winning home run.

3. Use crayons for a change of medium.

Variation for Higher Grades

Use watercolor instead of tempera paint on white paper for mood pictures that are realistic or color only.

Lesson Six: Yes, Just an Ordinary Sponge!

SPONGE PAINTING

You've painted with brushes—all kinds of brushes—you've painted with your fingers (that's fun, too), but have you ever painted with a sponge? Yes, just a plain, ordinary sponge like you'd use at the kitchen sink! What will you paint? Well, almost anything, but this time let's paint some fruit, simple things like apples, pears, bananas. Have some real or artificial fruit to look at. Talk about the roundness of it, the variations in colors. Notice that both sides aren't necessarily exactly the same shape.

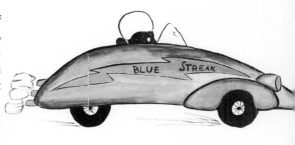

Then think of what a piece of sponge (cut to about 1½ x 2½ inches) is like. Do you think you could paint tiny details with it? Well—probably not. It's much more bulky than a brush. So we'll have to think of just trying to get the big, important shape of the fruit.

But with a sponge it's easy to make the fruit look round. Just sweep the sponge in a rounding line, like the edge of the fruit. Try the motion in the air—make it big, and move your hand rapidly in a swinging motion.

Now let's try the sponges on paper and see what happens. Have the pieces of sponges dampened but all the water squeezed out. In addition to a sponge, give each person a small piece of paper (about 6 x 9 to act as a palette) and put a little puddle of tempera paint on it—any color will do for now. Lightly press the flat side of the sponge into the puddle of paint. Remove some of the paint by patting the sponge gently against the palette paper several times. Then, on a practice piece of manila or white drawing paper (9 x 12 will do), try making several rounding strokes. Hold the sponge loosely and touch the paper lightly. Don't try to make a solid, brush-like line, but let the background paper show through to give a textured quality typical of a sponge. Repeat several times until the desired effect is achieved. Then try gradually straightening the lines. Whenever more paint is needed, repeat the process of touching the puddle of paint with the sponge, then lightly dabbing it onto the palette to remove the excess paint.

On the same practice paper try painting the outside shape of an apple. Then gradually straighten the line as it comes in to the center from each side. Looks round, almost three-dimensional, doesn't it?

Now you should be ready to sponge paint whichever kind of fruit you'd like. Look at each one carefully, again noticing basic shape. Let each child throw away or keep his practice paper, whichever he chooses. Lightly fold the used palette papers in half and drop in the wastebasket as it is passed. The sponges shouldn't need any washing. If a different basic color is to be used from the one used on the practice paper, simply turn the sponge over to the opposite side—and there it is, a clean surface again. Pass out fresh painting papers, either 12 x 18 white drawing or manila. Also, pass out new palette papers and give each child his choice of red or yellow, depending on which fruit he chooses to paint. As soon as each child has his necessary materials, let him begin.

Look at the shape. Hold the sponge lightly and paint with a swinging motion. Don't press too hard! Let the paper show through. Now gradually make the lines straighter as they come toward the center. Make it look round. That's good! Don't paint too much!

Then stop and look again at the fruit. Probably there's a suggestion of a second color on the apple or pear or banana. Maybe the apple is mostly red but has a touch of green on it, or perhaps it has a little yellow on it. Don't worry about the stem or leaf—that will come later.

Give each child the tiniest dab of whatever second color he needs to complete his fruit. Be sparing when you paint the second color. Remember, it's just an accent. Paint it in the same direction as the first color, depending upon where it is placed. Use the same side of the sponge and let it blend with the original paint, or if a completely fresh color is desired, turn the sponge to an unused side.

Now let's give it a stem. To get a fine, stem-like line simply dip the corner of the sponge in the paint, dab off most of it, and make a short, quick rounding line coming from the top of the fruit. Probably you'll want a speck of brown on the palette for that. Add a leaf, if you'd like. Look at the shape of the apple leaf or pear leaf, then paint it.

One piece of fruit all by itself is less interesting than two together. So how about pretending that there's a second, different kind of fruit partly in back of the first one. Then just paint the part that would show. Perhaps you'd like to place several pairs of fruit together about the room to give the idea.

Don't overpaint! Stop—stop—stop when it looks just right. Use a watercolor brush to sketch the outline of the fruit. Dip the brush into thin black tempera paint, remove most of it so that the brush is pointed, and SKETCH around the outside of each piece of fruit. This will make the whole picture stand out more clearly.

Collect the sponges for washing later, lightly fold the palette papers and put them in the wastebasket as it is passed, and you're all ready to inspect the results of a new painting experience.

Use the paper cutter to trim the finished pictures to better fit the background paper (if need be), and mount the sponge-painted pictures on a piece of black construction paper so as to be like the sketched line in the painting. Have the black paper only a tiny bit bigger than the painting, less than a quarter inch all around. A larger mounting would overpower the delicacy of the sponge technique. As always, add to the value of the lesson by displaying the finished pictures.

Make It Easy—for Yourself!

1. Use a pair of scissors or a mat knife to cut ordinary kitchen sponges into four parts.
2. Wet the sponges and squeeze out all the water before it is time for the lesson.

3. Use disposable palettes (any paper about 6 x 9) for an easy cleanup.
4. Use plastic detergent bottles for an easy way to distribute tempera paint.
5. Place fruit in several parts of the room so that it can be easily seen by all in the class.

Variations

1. Paint on colored construction paper for an interesting background.
2. Make a still life arrangement and make a painting of it using sponges.
3. Make a landscape painting using a sponge in place of a brush.

Variations for Lower Grades

1. Use sponges as experimental tools. Try lightly pressing them flat on a paper as well as stroking with them. Use several colors and develop a non-objective picture from these experiments.
2. Make simple object pictures—flowers, animals, birds. Use the simple pressing and painting techniques without attempting to make the objects look round.
3. Use sponges to paint any pictures the children would ordinarily paint with brushes.

Variations for Higher Grades

1. Make a still life arrangement of autumn fruits. Stress important elements in an interesting arrangement—height, balance, variety of size, overlapping. Work for a three-dimensional effect. Use colored construction paper for an attractive background color.
2. Paint a landscape with sponges, or a combination of brushes and sponges. Try to get a three-dimensional quality to the picture.
3. Use sponges to paint with watercolor for a change of medium.

Lesson Seven: Who Needs a Brush!

PAINTING WITH SWAB STICKS

You've painted with a brush, of course, but who needs a brush! Have you ever painted with a swab stick? Probably not. They're a novelty, but they're also lots of fun and a wonderful tool for getting children to experiment.

Begin by making it clear that this is a chance to experiment, to try out something different and find out just what can be done with it. Try using the side of the swab stick, the tip of it, press down on it, use it lightly—any way you can think of. Remember it is a new tool, so try to use it in as many ways as possible.

Divide the class time into two periods. The first is for pure experimentation, not for trying to make any kind of finished picture. Give each child a piece of 9 x 12 white drawing paper, one or two swab sticks, and a small piece of paper (for a palette) with several little dabs of different colors of tempera paint on it. Encourage each person to see how many different ways he can think of to use the swab sticks.

Walk around the room observing what is happening. Whenever you see someone has done something a little bit different, make a comment about it. "That's good! That's different from what anyone else has done." "That's different, too! I wonder if anyone else will think of using the swab stick that way." Comments such as these not only please the child whose work you comment about, but they encourage the others to experiment and to be different. Reassure them frequently by reminding them not to worry about what these papers look like, that they can be thrown away later.

If some in the class are hesitant to try a variety of ways of working with the swab sticks, ask some questions that may suggest new ideas to them. "Could you print with the swab sticks as well as brush with them?" "What happens when you press on hard? Is it different from when you use the swab stick lightly?" "How about using two colors at once? Could you do that?"

After about 15 minutes of experimentation, share all the ideas. Encourage each child to tell how he got a certain effect. Ask if anyone else discovered the same way of using the swab stick. Quickly go on to another new idea.

When all the ways that were found to use swab sticks have been shared, allow the children to throw away the experiment paper if they wish. Some may want to keep them. Collect any swab sticks and palette papers that are no longer usable. Replace these with fresh supplies.

Ask each child to think of a picture he would like to paint with swab sticks. Perhaps only one technique will be used—or perhaps two or three or even more of the experiments will be needed to complete the picture. Let each child decide whether he wants his picture to be realistic or not. Each child should choose either 9 x 12 or 12 x 18 white drawing paper, depending on what his picture and techniques will be. Then go to work.

The clean-up at the end of the period is no problem at all. There is nothing to wash. Simply have each child put his used swab sticks on the palette paper and drop the whole thing in the wastebasket as someone passes it around the room. As that is being done, each child prints his name at the bottom of the picture (or some appropriate place on the picture) with pencil, and then each child is ready to share his painting with the rest of the class.

As this is basically an experimentation lesson, it is important even while sharing finished pictures to stress originality of technique.

Display the finished pictures—and perhaps some of the first experiments—with an appropriate title.

Make It Easy—for Yourself!

1. Have an ample supply of swab sticks. Some children will need only two or three—others may need more.
2. Use regular commercial swab sticks or make your own by twisting a bit of cotton batting at each end of an applicator stick about four inches long.
3. Do not use pencils for any drawing.
4. Do not attempt to wash swab sticks. Throw them away.
5. Use each end of the swab stick for a different color.
6. Have a choice of either 9 x 12 or 12 x 18 paper for the finished painting.
7. Plastic detergent bottles make excellent containers for storing and dispensing tempera paint.
8. Use small pieces of old paper about 6 x 9 for disposable palettes. Paper that is faded or that has thumb tack holes in it is fine for this.
9. Very little paint is needed for this type of work so distribute only small dabs of needed colors.
10. For an easy clean-up have each child put all his used swab sticks on the palette paper, fold it over lightly to keep the extra paint from spilling, and drop it all in the wastebasket as it is passed around the room.

Variations

1. Use swab sticks in place of brushes—but to make the types of paintings which they have made before and which they are familiar with: landscapes, abstract or non-objective painting, blended colors, portraits.
2. Use with transparent watercolors instead of tempera paint.

Variations for Lower Grades

1. Use longer applicators for younger children.
2. Use in place of brushes for regular type pictures. In this case the experimental purpose of the lesson is more incidental than it is with older children.

WATER COLOR

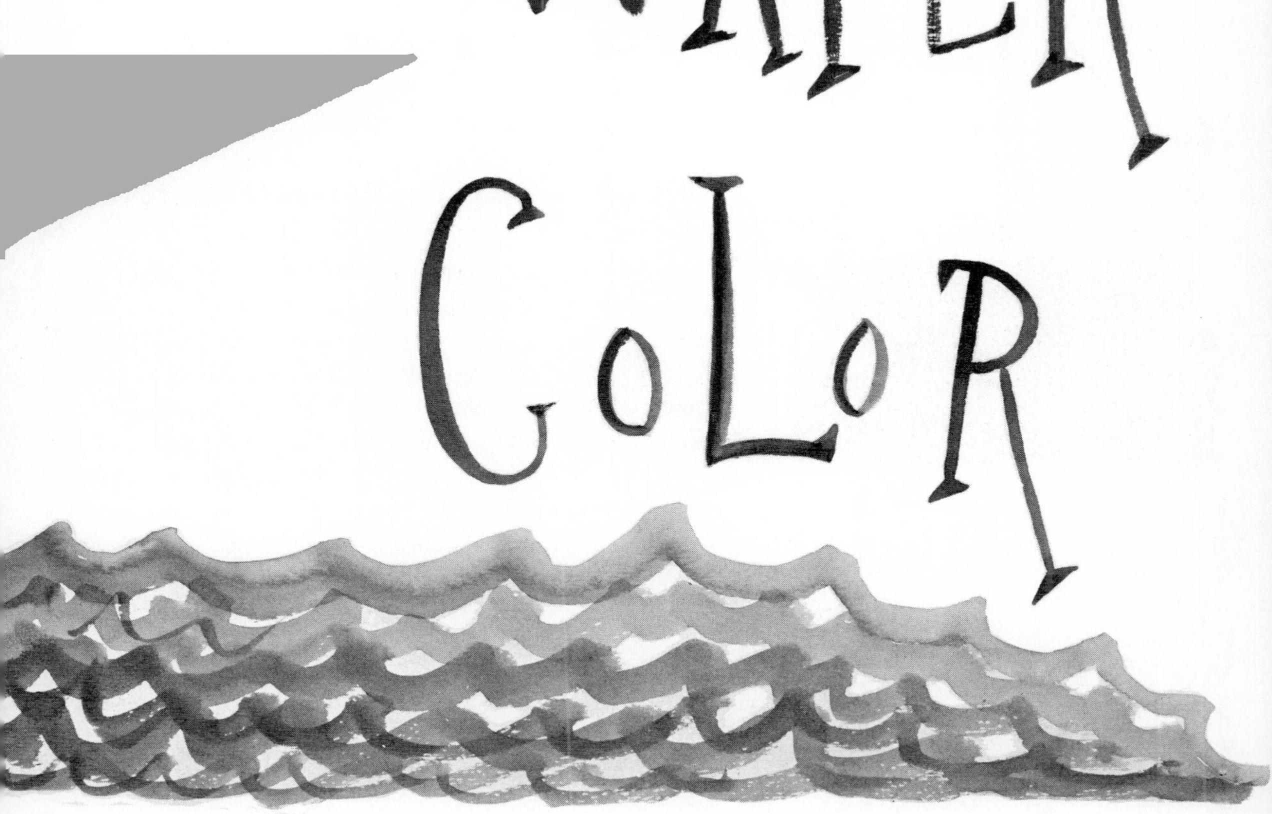

CHAPTER **2**

Water Color

Lesson One: Top of the Ladder

WATER COLOR TECHNIQUES

SUCCESS IS AT THE TOP OF THE LADDER, BUT YOU can't start there, particularly with water color. So let's climb the ladder, one rung at a time. Each rung of our ladder will be a water color technique. You've noticed how enthusiastic children are when they get their first box of water colors. Now mix that enthusiasm with enough skill to gain success at the top of the ladder.

Have the class gather around you in a large semi-circle while you present a short demonstration. Oh, yes, you *can* do it! You'll even glow with pride when you hear the admiring exclamations.

30

Begin by making a *flat wash*. Get a large brush full of paint—any color you like. Hold a piece of 9 x 12 white drawing paper so that the top of it is slightly off the desk. Quickly spread a band of paint across part of the paper near the top. Immediately overlap the bottom edge of the paint as you lay on another band of the same color. Repeat this several times until a desired area is covered. By tipping the paper the color has drained down to the bottom edge of the wet paint and will blend evenly with the next band when it is overlapped. Wipe the surplus paint from the brush onto the newspaper and finish the flat wash by drawing the brush across the bottom edge of paint, picking up the extra paint with the now dry brush. How flat and smooth the whole area looks! What does it make you think of? The flat side of a house, certainly—or any flat, even surface.

Use another part of the same paper for a *graded wash* this time. Use the same color as before, or try a different one if you like. Tip the paper and put a band of color across the upper part, the same as you did before. But this time quickly dip the brush in the jar of water (just dip, don't wash), then overlap the same as before and lay on another band of paint. Again dip the brush in the water and repeat the process of overlapping to paint a band of color—dipping, and again painting several times. Pick up the surplus paint and water at the bottom edge the same as you did before. The area painted doesn't look flat as it did last time, but it is graded and gets lighter as it goes lower on the paper. Why? Of course, the more water the lighter the paint. Makes it look as though it goes way back into the distance. Certainly, it would be a wonderful way to make a sky.

But let's try something very different on another section of your dry paper. Dip the side of your brush into one color, then quickly turn it and dip the other side into a different color. Paint a strip of color on an empty place and see what happens! The two colors have partially blended. What could you paint that way with a *blended brush* stroke? Grass would be fine—or anything that is blended.

This time dip your brush into one color, then just the tip of the brush into a different color. Don't spread the paint as you have done before, just lay the brush flat on the paper. The colors that were at the end of the brush have blended. Looks like a petal—or put several together into a mass. Maybe it could be foliage on a tree, or water, depending on the colors you used. You can do lots of things with a *tipped brush*. Try using a light tone with a darker color on the tip. Then paint with the side of your brush for a shaded effect.

Now one more technique—*dry brush*. This time wipe most of the paint off the brush onto the newspaper. When the brush is almost dry, spread it across the paper. Notice how the paint skips over some areas and touches the paper in other places. Yes, it does look like grass, or perhaps another color could be sand, or even shadows.

All the way from very wet painting to very dry painting—and in only 10 minutes! Everyone will be eager to try the techniques on his own—materials, time, and encouragement are all that are needed.

For the next 10 or 15 minutes let each child try the same techniques you demonstrated. Some of the techniques they will want to try several times to get the real feel of them. Then make one suggestion, for this time only: try using all five techniques to make one picture. Pass out clean paper and watch imagination go to work.

Make this learning experience have added value by making a display showing each of the various techniques. Cut out sections of each paper that shows an especially successful experiment, group them according to the techniques they show, and label each group. Not only will it be a display the class will be proud of, but it will serve as a reminder of what they have learned, and be an excellent motivation for the next lesson. The display will also show that they have begun to climb the ladder of success.

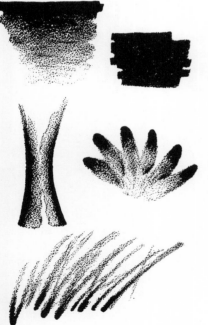

Make It Easy—for Yourself!

1. Cover all work areas with newspaper.
2. Watercolor materials can be cleaned easily. Each child should have a piece of soft cotton cloth (as from a worn-out sheet or pillowcase) for cleaning supplies. a) Wash brush in jar of water and wipe lightly on cloth; b) use cloth to wipe out any paint or water that has gotten into the box of paints; c) empty jar (or pan) of water and dry with the cloth—no washing will be necessary if it is wiped out immediately.
3. If there is no sink in the classroom, have two pails—one with clean water and one for dirty water.
4. Use watercolor brushes as large as possible—nothing smaller than #8, and larger wash brushes if they are available.

Lesson Two: Splash, Magic, and Imagination

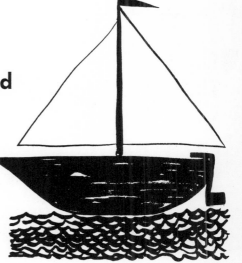

WET WATER COLOR PAINTING

SPLASH! AN EXPLOSION OF COLOR. MAGIC! NEW colors appear. Imagination! making something from nothing. These are the elements of an art lesson which will bring forth "oohs" and "ahs" from your class.

To show the importance of using water as the controlling factor in the use of transparent watercolors, try this imaginative lesson. Begin as usual with the distribution of materials, making sure that work areas are well covered with newspaper or another absorbing material.

If they are available, use large #12 wash brushes. If there are none

33

of these, regular brushes found in the sets may be used. Since this lesson is highly visual, the best motivation is a teacher demonstration. Don't worry about having no skill because this technique is so basic it can be done by anyone.

Start by putting a drop of clear water on each color so they will be ready to use. Next, with your large brush, paint the surface of the paper with clear water, wetting the entire surface. Use a lot of water but avoid puddles. Push the excess off the paper onto the newspaper. Quickly fill your brush with one of the primary colors (red, yellow, or blue), again using a lot of water, and touch the wet paper with the point of the brush.

Splash! an explosion of color will radiate out. Continue placing this same color on the paper, always working quickly. For the most dramatic effect, begin with red. Wash out your brush between colors and repeat the process with the other two primary colors. Magic! the secondary colors will appear (orange, green, and purple). The result will be a non-objective composition of brilliant colors.

Now have the class create their own explosive designs. Caution them about deep puddles and remind them to overlap the primary colors to create the secondary ones.

Our explosive designs can also be used to create highly decorative and fanciful pictures. Using black construction paper or any dark color, an image is cut out carefully. Instead of using the positive cut out shape, mount the black paper with the cut out negative area on top of the watercolor design. If, for example, a fish is cut out of the construction paper which is then mounted on the watercolor paper, we have created a multi-color fanciful tropical fish. Eyes, fins, and other decoration cut out of the black paper may be added for a more finished design.

This can also be done in reverse. That is, an image can be cut out of the watercolor design and pasted on a dark background, adding the details once again for a more finished product. All you need is a splash, a little magic, and lots of imagination!

Make It Easy—for Yourself!

1. Cover all work areas with newspaper.
2. Watercolor materials can be cleaned easily. Each child should have a piece of soft cotton cloth (as from a worn-out sheet or pillowcase) for cleaning supplies. a) Wash brush in a jar of water and wipe lightly on cloth; b) use cloth to wipe out any paint or water that has gotten into

the box of paints; c) empty jar (or pan) of water and dry with the cloth—no washing will be necessary if it is wiped out immediately.

3. If there is no sink in the classroom, have two pails—one with clean water and one for dirty water.

4. Use watercolor brushes as large as possible—nothing smaller than #8, and larger wash brushes if they are available.

Variations

1. Have the class paint actual scenes on wet paper. The results will be quite unusual and have an unreal quality. The painting must be done quickly, therefore more than one can be done in a period. With practice, the class will discover the limitations of this technique and omit details. Themes which are appropriate to the fuzzy-like result are more desirable. For example, this technique is good for suggesting cloudy days, storms, fog, and twilight pictures.

2. Have the class paint pictures which only have part of the paper wet, showing how wet painting can be used within a composition—such as a wet area for a sunset, or as foliage of a tree, or for a lake or a river, or anything else that calls for blended colors.

3. Using our designs as colorful backgrounds, scenes cut from black paper are pasted across the bottom of the colored sheet. These designs sometimes resemble sunsets, exploding fireworks, outer space, and many other backgrounds. Using the inspiration of the background, let each child work out a picture in silhouette, whether it is a city scene, a country landscape, or a rocket in space. Childlike imagination can come up with amazing and varied results.

4. Ask your class if they've ever tried to find realistic figures and shapes in the clouds. This is the basic idea involved with our wet painting. Using the smaller brush and black paint, have the class try to find objects in the designs and outline them with a narrow line. Small details, such as eyes, mouth, and buttons, may be added to the found objects. You will be amazed at the number of images your students will discover when you encourage them. This lesson also is excellent practice in the use of the brush for detailed work.

OBJECTIVES

1. **To provide experience with watercolors.**

2. **To use watercolor in a realistic picture, using the medium in a free, fluid manner.**

3. **To have experience organizing a simple painting, leaving out distracting detail.**

4. **To provide opportunity for blending watercolors and for using appropriate watercolor techniques to obtain desired effects.**

(For grades 5 and 6, adapted to grades 3 and 4)

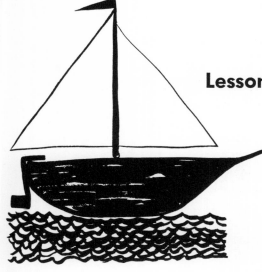

Lesson Three: Well, Let's Paint Them!

WATER COLOR LANDSCAPE PAINTING

YOU'VE SEEN A TALL, GRACEFUL TREE, ITS GREEN foliage silhouetted against the clear, light blue sky. A low, rolling mountain range stretches across the horizon. You wished you could paint it. It would make a lovely picture—quiet, relaxing. You've watched an approaching storm, the sky heavy with gray clouds, thickening to an angry blue-black. A nearby tree bent slightly as it resisted the wind rushing through its branches. Even the abandoned shack in the distance looked dark and forbidding. A dramatic though intense moment. You'd like to paint it.

Well, let's paint them! Watercolor will be an ideal medium, for in describing each scene you've already eliminated all but the essentials —and that's a good thing to do with watercolor, too.

For a moment think of your watercolor picture as just a design in which you break up the area into several spaces, each a different size. Make them fill all of a 9 x 12 or 12 x 18 sheet of white drawing paper. One will eventually be the sky. Then, in the first, quiet picture there will be a narrow irregular area for the rolling mountains. To one side of the paper will be a tall, vertical line beginning near the bottom of the paper and extending upward and branching outward well up into the sky area. Do this much with the lightest tint of blue or grey watercolor. Just sketch in the lines for a guide. Keep those lines light. They're not really a part of the picture; they're just to help you later on. You may even want to change them some. So keep them *light*! Already you have a good beginning.

Or perhaps you want to make the more dramatic picture—the storm. Begin the same way: a very light tint of blue or grey water-color to sketch in a *big* area for the sky. That will be the most important part of your picture, so keep it big; it will be divided into smaller storm clouds later. Then the shack in the distance: just a rectangular area with a roof, perhaps extending slightly into the part which will be the sky. Then, to one side and beginning near the bottom of the paper, extending upward and leaning slightly into the center of the paper, sketch a vertical line. Branch it so that it points toward the center of the paper—the beginning of a storm-swept tree. All you need for a good beginning.

Or think of any landscape or seascape. Divide the paper into mainly horizontal areas: sky; water; mountains; a peninsula of land pointing out into the water; a rolling land area overlapping another, flatter land area; a row of buildings close together in a street scene. Then add height to your areas. Perhaps those buildings add height as well as a long line; or a cluster of trees; or a graceful sail from a tiny boat; or anything you can think of. Think of your own picture and keep it simple; plan the areas—vary the sizes. Sketch them *lightly* with watercolor.

Now think of what you know about color. Which are more interesting—harsh colors right from the box with no variety, or blended colors you make that have endless variety? No doubt about it, is there? So think of the colors you will use. The light delicate blue with lots of water or the threatening grey sky, boiling with heavier blues and dark grey. Think of the mountain range that tells you it is far in the distance, because of its hazy blues and purples, with darker blues and purples falling as shadows always on one side. Think how you can make a variety of greens for the foliage against the light sky —some of the greens with extra yellow, some with extra blue. Or think of the dull and dark greens blowing in the storm—red added to some of the green to dull it or black added to darken it. Think *color,* blended color, contrast of color (dark against light—light next to dark).

Then think of the watercolor techniques you know: wet paper technique, the color spread by the water; flat and graded washes; blended brush; tipped brush; dry brush. Think which of these techniques you want to use to create various effects. Perhaps a graded wash for the clear sky, perhaps wet paper for the storm sky. Think what you want each part to look like. Which technique will give you that effect?

Now you have your picture planned, the areas sketched. You know what colors to blend. You know what techniques to use. So—let's paint! Be loose and free with it. Don't worry about it—good space arrangement plus blended colors will make an interesting picture regardless of anything else. So loosen up and paint rapidly.

No! No! No! Don't resort to outlining and just filling in! Oh, that would be so flat and dull.

Back to blending colors, working on the whole area at one time. Lots of water. Make that brush move with easy, gliding motions. Remember to have strong contrasts of color. Get something dark up against that light area. Now something light touching all that dark area.

Stop for a minute and let the paint dry if you don't want those colors to run together. You know, wet paint on wet paper will run whether you want it to or not. So relax a while and wait. Or work on another area and then come back to that first section later. Don't paint too much. When it looks just right, leave it alone—it's finished!

Put the papers to one side to dry. (They're apt to curl and warp some as any wet paper will do, but that won't do any harm when they are dry and are displayed.) Clean up the easy way—as described later.

When you come back and look at those paintings you'll be amazed.

They're much better than you thought they were while they were being painted. Why they don't look the same at all! Display them. Even improve them further in the process of displaying them: use the paper cutter to trim or crop them if needed; mat some or just mount them on a white background. (A light picture may be improved by giving it a very narrow band of darker color before mounting it on white paper.) They look good, don't they?

Make It Easy—for Yourself!

1. Have all work areas covered with newspaper.
2. Have all watercolor materials ready before the beginning of the lesson. (Watercolor boxes, jars or pans for individual water containers, large watercolor brushes, cotton rags for cleaning up.)
3. No pencils—do sketching of areas with *light* paint.
4. Give children a choice of 9 x 12 or 12 x 18 white drawing paper. Some children feel more comfortable painting either larger or smaller than other children.
5. Encourage children to think through their pictures before doing any painting. Changes can be made, of course, but a good plan is a good beginning.
6. Encourage rapid and free painting, not being concerned about details.
7. Keep the pictures simple.
8. Permit—even *encourage*—children to stand while painting. It encourages using the brush loosely and lightly and permits more freedom of motion!
9. Hold the brush at or near the end of the handle. Only for the tiniest of details does the brush need to be held as a pencil—and these are to be avoided as much as possible in watercolor work.
10. Clean up the easy way. Each person washes his brush in his own water container, then wipes it on his cotton rag. This draws out even dirty water. Use rag to wipe out and clean the watercolor box. Empty water containers into the sink (or pail) and wipe the container at once with the rag. Have one person collect and store each of the basic supplies: boxes and brushes, water containers. Rags may be saved for the next lesson.

Variations

1. Have other lessons that are similar except for choice of subject matter: landscapes, seascapes, still life.

2. Paint pictures that illustrate the various moods of a place —for example: downtown street on a sale day; downtown street during a blizzard; downtown street on Sunday afternoon; downtown street during a parade; downtown street when it is raining.

3. Show slides of various places you or the children have been. Talk about what they would paint if they were actually there. What would they leave out of their paintings? What would they include? How would they break up the space for the beginning? After looking at many pictures and talking about them, have the children make their own paintings.

4. Look at many slides of one place. Try to get the mood of the place. Then paint a picture that will capture the same atmosphere.

5. Go outdoors and paint something you actually see. Don't try to put in every detail, but choose the most important parts. Have the painting papers taped to a drawing board (a large, heavy cardboard works fine). Distribute the water from a pail once the class is outside. Water from containers can be disposed of outside.

6. Think of your picture as areas of color rather than as specific objects. Paint in the colors, filling the whole paper. When the paint is dry, sketch the objects, represented by color, with a dark color on the brush. Use very fine lines and sketch rather than draw. Don't worry that the sketched lines don't entirely match the color areas— they shouldn't.

Variations for Lower Grades

1. Use tempera paint rather than watercolor. Use slides as motivation.

2. Paint outdoors with tempera paint.

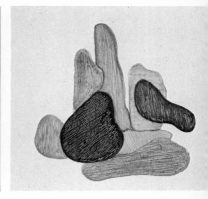

Lesson Four: But See—That's an Elephant!

TEXTURED WATER COLOR

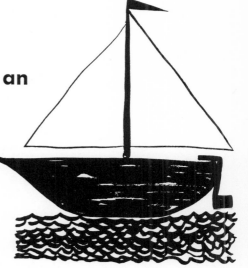

So you thought they were just areas of color —lovely ones, to be sure—but nothing more! But, see —that's an elephant standing on his hind legs, or it's balloons, or Puss'n Boots, or a dog begging.

Children give wonderfully imaginative titles to their water color abstracts. That's even an important part of it, for creativeness doesn't begin with a paint brush and end when it is laid down. But, back to the watercolor abstracts.

One of the most important things to do to make more interesting water color paintings is to blend colors. So let's do that today, not getting involved at all with trying to make anything that looks real. Begin by assembling the usual water color materials: paint box of

41

colors, jars or pans of water, paint brushes, 9 x 12 white drawing paper, and pieces of cloth for cleanup. Talk for a few minutes about what colors do to each other: black always darkens a color; water thins the color and makes it look lighter; opposite colors grey each other; red and yellow make orange; red and blue make purple; blue and yellow make green. Then show how to blend colors into interesting abstracts.

Gather the class about you in a big semi-circle and demonstrate how to proceed. Near the center (never exactly in the middle) of a 9 x 12 white drawing paper, paint a large free-form shape with any color you want. Let's say it was blue. Immediately, while the blue paint is still wet, add just a tiny bit of black to it and repaint the same area, blending it into the blue. See how it has darkened it. In another part of the paper repeat the first step—paint another area of blue. Make it a different size and shape for variety. Quickly dip the brush into a new color, perhaps green this time. Paint right over the second blue area. A new kind of blue, this time with a greenish tinge. Each blue area is different and each a more interesting color than the original one that came from the box.

About now try something new—add *texture* to the painted areas. To do this, simply reverse the way you hold the brush. Have the pointed end of the handle down, and with it in this position scratch into the painted areas, making the scratch lines very close together and all in the same direction. Cover the whole area with these marks, then move to the second painted area but this time turn the paper so that all the scratch marks will go in a different direction.

Why scratch into the paint? Two reasons: they make a more interesting effect than without them, and it is a good technique to be able to use in other watercolor paintings. For example, it is a wonderful way to indicate tall grass without trying to paint in each delicate line. Or it's a fine way to show the roughness of bark on a tree.

But now back to the painting. Try a new color this time. If it is red, paint it on a new area just as it comes from the box. Then add its opposite, green. See what has happened! A softer, greyer red, much more pleasing than the hard original color. Try red again, this time changing it in some other way. Remember to always add texture before the paint has dried.

Continue this way until all of the 9 x 12 paper is covered with textured colors. Try to give as much variety to the color as possible, for this is a learning experience in the blending of colors. At the same time try to balance colors, making an interesting color arrangement.

When the paintings are finished have each child hold his up in the air, as far away from him as possible, and turn it in all directions. Which way looks the best? What does it remind you of? Give it a title—an imaginative title that will be as interesting as the painting itself. Have each child write his title on the back of the picture so that when you display the textured watercolors you can put the titles with them. That will make the experience more meaningful to the child and the results more meaningful to the observer.

Make It Easy—for Yourself!

1. Cover all work areas with newspaper. It makes it easier to paint all the way to the edges of the paper—and insures a quicker cleanup.
2. Use large watercolor brushes, at least #8 and preferably larger wash brushes.
3. Have paint rags (pieces of old sheet or pillowcase, each about a foot square) to wipe out paint boxes and water containers. With this type of cleanup no washing is necessary.
4. No pencils!

Variations

1. Follow the same procedure except do not cover all of the paper. Stop at any point when the picture looks finished: good placement on the paper, color balanced, idea seems complete.
2. Work out various specific color problems: all variations of one color only; all light colors; all dark colors; all dull colors; specific color combinations.

Variation for Lower Grades

Use tempera paint on newsprint, blending colors in the same way. Texturing can not be done on newsprint as the paper would tear. It might be done, however, if the painting is done on manila paper.

OBJECTIVES

1. To have further experience with watercolor as a medium.

2. To use color to interpret moods.

3. To study placing of facial features.

4. To enjoy watercolor in a fun experience.

(For grades 5 and 6, adapted to grades 3 and 4)

Lesson Five: All in One Picture!

MOOD PORTRAITS

ARE YOU ALWAYS IN A GOOD MOOD? OR SOMETIMES do you feel angry? Or are you ever unhappy or just blue? Well, most of us are! We're really always the same person, but we don't always act like the same person—or even look the same!

Let's paint ourselves in our various moods, all in one picture! We'll use watercolor, so cover all the work areas with newspaper and assemble the necessary materials: watercolor boxes, water containers for each person, cotton rags, large watercolor brushes, and 12 x 18 white drawing paper. We'll also need black wax crayons.

44

Think about color for a moment. When you are blue you are ——?
Unhappy, of course! But if things are rosy you are ——? Just the
opposite, you are happy. If you are green you are probably in a jealous
mood. If things look grey to you, you are ——? That's right—sad,
lonely. If you're excited, things are looking pretty bright, perhaps
orange. Or are you purple with rage?

Well, you have the idea! Color expresses mood, so later we'll
emphasize several different colors and see ourselves in several different
moods.

But first of all, what do you really look like? Do you have a long
face or a round one? Do you have a pointed chin or a square one? Do
you have curly hair or straight hair? This must be *you*, remember!

With a dark crayon (black is a good color), lightly draw in the
oval for your face—a long oval or a fat oval. Make it *your* face, *your*
chin. Make it just a thin outline—don't fill in anything. Sketch in
the way your hair looks. Do your ears show? The boy's ears will, of
course. Now for the eyes. Watch where you put them! They're just
half way down your head, you know. Don't get them too high! Now
the rest of the features—the eyebrows, the mouth, and nose.

Go over the light lines you have just drawn. Darken them with a
heavy black crayon line. Make the outline look just like you.

Decide which moods you'll show. Maybe you'll want to think of
how you felt or acted at different times during the past week. Then
quickly with your brush apply those colors. Divide the face into four
or five parts, each painted with a different color. If you've been happy
most of the time, make that the biggest area. If it's been a bad week
for you, show that by making that the largest area. But cover the
whole face. Let each section dry before letting another color touch it
so that they won't run together.

When the face has all been painted in various colors to show the
several moods you've been in lately, do the same thing with all the
background area. Divide it into several areas and paint them with
different colors. Use a dry brush technique if you like so that some
of the white paper shows through. It will add an interesting texture
to the area.

And there you are! Just one of you but in several moods. Didn't
know you looked that way, did you?

They'll make a wonderful display that will provoke lots of con-
versation. Be ready to answer questions—or better yet, let your class
do that for you.

Make It Easy—for Yourself!

1. Cover all work areas with newspaper.
2. Have painting materials ready before the art lesson begins: watercolor boxes, large watercolor brushes, jars or pans for water for each person, cotton rags, two pails (if there is no sink in the room)—one for clean water and one to empty dirty water into.
3. Encourage children to let each color dry before letting another color touch it. Otherwise, the colors will run together.
4. Talk with class about the shape of the face and where the features are placed before they begin sketching their own faces. (Eyes half way down the head; nose half way between eyes and chin; mouth about half way between nose and chin; ears from eyebrows to tip of nose.)

Variations

1. Use watercolor to paint other mood pictures: the saddest (happiest, angriest) person I ever saw; the angry sea; the threatening storm.
2. Use color and line only to create an abstract of a mood in watercolor.

Variations for Lower Grades

1. Use tempera paint to paint a picture of yourself when you're happy and another one of yourself when you're sad.
2. Use just color and line to create a mood that is angry, excited, happy, or lazy.

CHAPTER **3**   *Fingerpainting*

Lesson One: Little Fingers Itch

FINGERPAINTING—RHYTHM DESIGNS

How would you like to fingerpaint? If you ask that question of your class—*any* class—just be prepared for the most enthusiastic response you've ever had. All children love to fingerpaint! Their little fingers practically itch to get into the soft, gooey paint.

So let's make some preparations, for nothing else is as important for insuring the lessons's success. Begin by asking each child to bring in an old shirt which his father has thrown away. This will make the best cover-up protection possible. Cut off the sleeves near the shoulders, put the shirt on backwards, fasten the top button or two and you have an ideal "insurance" against accidents.

Also, as part of the preparations, be sure you have a large supply of newspapers. They will be used for a thorough covering of all work areas as well as being put on the floor so that wet paintings can be layed on them to dry.

A paper towel for each child, cans for water, an assortment of of fingerpaint, and fingerpaint paper and you are all set. No cial equipment is necessary. A sink and big tables are fine required.

lesson with a short demonstration. You'll have fun paint-the class will learn from it. First, how do you prepare the side of the paper, you notice, is shiny. Have that side now have the paper well back on the desk or table so that n on nt will spill onto the floor. Then take a can of water erent e puddle of water in the center of the paper. Lay the and flat in the water and quickly spread it evenly over lide, er. Be sure all of the paper is thoroughly wet. If you over ugh water add more. Oops! this is too much, so just I'll o right off the sides onto the newspaper. Don't splash ttom push it off. it it e fun! Dip your fingers into the jar of fingerpaint and for t a tablespoonful. Lay it in the center of the paper, just h the water. Put your hand flat on the paint and stir it ully times until it feels smooth. (Oh, it feels soft and good! oor. e feel of it.) Then spread it out over the whole paper ger- d with the water, letting it go right off the edges onto been r. Your hand should slide easily over the paper. If it iate that shows that the paper is too dry—so quickly add a the ater, mix the whole thing and spread it over the paper. is thin, add more paint so that the whole thing is a rich up, ft, smooth consistency. ed, notice where I'm standing? Way back from the table, int- nough for someone to walk in front of me. This is for so that I will stay clean, and, even more important, it is tter nt that way. See, if I move up close to the table I can't all rm easily, but if I step back again, lean over and support my left hand on the table, then I can move my right for rm easily. So stay way back when you paint.

Make your hand into a tight fist and, pressing down on the fleshy part, move your hand rhythmically all the way across the paper in big circular motions. Then drop down a little lower and repeat the same motion across the paper. Whatever motion you start with, continue it over and over again until the whole paper is covered with a rhythmic repeat pattern. Then "erase" the whole thing by rubbing your hand over all of it.

Could you use any other motions? Well, let's see. You could hold your hand in a fist but move it differently: up and down in sharp points close together or in wider "V" shapes, in scallops or upside down scallops, and—well, you can think of other ways. You could also hold your hand in other ways, too, couldn't you? Try holding your hand open, resting upright on the little finger and side. the same motions as before, but see how differently they look that you are holding your hand differently. Try pressing down the side of your thumb and moving it in rhythmic motions. Diff again, aren't they?

Hold your hand any way you like, just make it glide, glide, g glide across the paper as if to music. Over and over and over and again. Make it cover the whole paper. See, it's finished! Now use my finger like a crayon to print my initials down at the bo corner. Oh, yes, your finger is like a crayon! It draws fine b can't paint—your hand does that much better. So, one hand painting and one finger for initials.

Pick your painting up by the corners closest to you and care lay it on the newspapers which have been spread out across the f

Now for the cleanup. Wipe off onto the paper towel all the fir paint you can get off your hand. (Only one hand should have in the paint.) You will be able to get enough off so that an immed washing won't be necessary. See, clean enough for now. Lay paper towel onto the dirty newspaper to be thrown away later.

At this point, the demonstration over, assign each person to a gr be sure all sleeves are pushed up, shirts are on backwards and butto and that everyone has remembered to stand way back from the p ing area.

Walk quickly about the room giving advice where needed. Be add more water, it's a little bit dry. That's the way, make sure it' wet.

But don't pause too long. Hurry to the other side of the room someone there will need your attention.

Be sure to stir the paint with your hand flat—then spread it out. Good! You're ready to paint. Make it glide easily. Pretend you're listening to music. Uh, uh! That's a crayon you're using! One finger is like a crayon. Remember? Use your whole hand.

And so on and on through the lesson. A quick reminder here, a word of praise there, another suggestion along the way.

With a whole class fingerpainting at one time, it is wise not to have anyone walking about the room with a wet fingerpainting except at your direction. So, as several people finish and put their initials at the bottom, supervise them—one or two at a time—as they carry their paintings and lay them on a newspaper on the floor.

As soon as each child has put his painting on the floor to dry, have him clean his hands (only one hand should have much paint on it) on his towel. When each person has finished, have one person in each group complete the clean-up—merely empty the cans of water and fold all the newspaper over and over and put them into a big container to be disposed of later. Easy! Make a quick inspection to see if there is a spot of paint anywhere on the floor or edge of desks or table. If so, let one person take a damp sponge and wipe it off.

The fingerpaintings will tend to curl a little, as will any wet paper. This will not cause any problem. When the paintings are completely dry, pile them together, and put something heavy on them if you like. But most important, display them—whether you have flattened them first or not. If the edges are rough, trim them slightly with a paper cutter. It will improve their appearance tremendously.

Last of all—make plans for another fingerpainting lesson soon! You'll want to, and your class will practically demand it.

Make It Easy—for Yourself!

1. Overlap at least two layers of newspaper on all working areas so that no paint or water will get on the desks or tables.
2. Be sure each person has an old shirt on backwards. A piece of string (or cotton roving) tied around the waist holds the shirt close to the body and makes it easier to work, especially when leaning over.
3. Arrange the room as you would for a tempera painting

lesson: four desks pushed together make a good table area, three children in a group, with a fourth desk used for supplies.

4. Have at least two small cans for water for each group. If more than three or four children are in a group you may want an extra can.

5. If you are working with little children (K through grade 3) you may want to cut the fingerpaint paper in half. Their short arms have room on the approximately 12 x 18 paper to make big rhythmic motions. In fact, the full-size paper may be so big for them that they find it difficult to reach all parts of it, and therefore are unable to work as freely as on a smaller paper.

6. Be sure children paint on the shiny side of the paper.

7. Have the room completely ready before the beginning of the lesson. Have a paper towel at each person's painting area. Have him put it under the newspaper so that he can slide it out easily at clean-up time. (Let him put it under the newspaper so he knows exactly where it is when needed.)

8. Yellow makes less contrast on the paper than other colors, so you may want to eliminate it if using only one color for a painting.

9. If chairs and desks are separate, move all the chairs to one side of the room. This will keep them clean, make it easier to paint, and have a place where the children may sit when they have finished painting, and will therefore make it easier to keep the lesson and the clean-up orderly. If the chairs are attached to the desks, have the children stand in back of the chairs to paint, and remain standing until all clean-up is finished.

10. Have children experiment with several positions of the hand and motions before settling on one.

11. Avoid "erasing" design more than a couple of times as there is less contrast in color with many "erasures."

12. Always stand to fingerpaint.

13. If the paper tends to move while you are working on it, lift one edge and put a *little* water underneath. That will hold the paper in place.

Variations

1. Blend two colors together. Blend them in areas only so as to produce a more varied and interesting color effect. Fingerpaint as before.

2. Make a design with wax crayons directly on the shiny surface of the fingerpaint paper. Then make a simple rhythmic fingerpainting over it.

3. Prepare the fingerpaint paper as for regular fingerpainting (water and paint spread over the surface). Then instead of painting with your hand, use some gadget such as the cover of a jar, edge of a piece of cardboard, tongue depressor, or cork to make the fingerpainting. The gadget may be printed (simply pressed into the wet paint) or it may be used with similar motions to those you would use with your hand.

4. Make a cardboard comb (by cutting V-shape notches at irregular intervals) and use on the prepared surface. They may be used in straight lines or in motions similar to those you did with your hand.

5. Make a monoprint from the original fingerpainting. A monoprint is made by laying another paper—it may be white drawing paper or colored construction paper—over the wet fingerpainting. Rub your hand over the back of the paper that is being printed, then peel it off the original painting. The monoprint will have a different texture than the original painting.

6. Prepare a paper for fingerpainting (water and paint). Then immediately lay another paper over it as if making a monoprint. Use any tool, such as the blunt end of a pencil, the point of a pencil, a tongue depressor (or any combination of them) to rub onto the back of the paper in the same rhythmic repeat designs as would be done on the fingerpaint itself. Pull the two papers apart. The result will be similar to a monoprint.

OBJECTIVES

1. **To provide further opportunity for working directly in a fluid material.**

2. **To continue to use fingerpaint with rhythmic, flowing motions.**

3. **To learn more about the technique of fingerpainting.**

4. **To produce a unit type of abstract fingerpainting.**

(For grades 4 through 6, adapted to grades 1 through 3)

Lesson Two: You Made a Promise!

FINGERPAINT ABSTRACTS

Do you remember how much your class enjoyed that last fingerpainting lesson? And you made a promise that they could fingerpaint again soon. So how about surprising them today!

Make the same careful preparations as you did the last time: newspapers, shirts, paper towels, fingerpaint paper and paints, cans of water. Arrange the room so that everything is all set before the lesson begins.

Then start with a short review of the important things already known about fingerpainting. That's right, one side of the paper is shiny and that's the side you paint on. A puddle of water on the paper first, spread it out making sure all of the paper is really wet. Yes, be sure to lay your hand flat on the scoop of paint and stir it until it is smooth before you spread it over the whole paper. Certainly you can add more water—or paint—if you need it. Good, I'm glad

56

you remembered to stand way back while you're painting. Lean over and balance yourself with one hand while you paint with the other. You'll do better to paint with only one hand, so keep the other one out of it. And most of all, paint with big, rhythmical motions.

Now for a quick demonstration. Have the class gather about you in a big circle. Prepare your paper with water and then the fingerpaint, again reviewing as you go along. Talk about the way you can hold your hand, the kinds of motions you can make.

But today we're going to do something a little bit different. Instead of making one or two kinds of motions over and over again, we're going to make a variety of motions—right on top of each other. What would happen, though, if we put a little motion down here near the bottom of the paper and then made a big one over it that went way to the top of the paper? Of course, it would "erase" most of that poor little thing! So instead we'll make a big, sweeping motion that goes all the way to the top—maybe some of it will go right on off the top of the paper. See!

Now let's start over again at the bottom of the paper—from the same spot as before—and make a different kind of motion, but not quite as tall this time. See, the top of the other one still shows and a different shape is in front of it.

Well, let's try again. Begin at the same spot, hold your hand differently, and make a different kind of rhythmic motion—but don't go quite as far up the paper. Each motion shows, doesn't it, and the design is getting prettier each time! Let's finish it. One or two more motions, each smaller and lower on the paper, but all beginning from the same point, and then—finished! Use your finger to print your name or initials on the bottom of the paper. Place the wet fingerpaint abstract on newspaper to dry, and then clean up.

When the paintings are dry, display them. You may find that if there is a rough edge to the paper you can improve the appearance of the picture by trimming it on a paper cutter. The finished abstracts will show to their full advantage if you mount them on a white paper with a rather wide border of several inches.

Remember, you promised!

Make It Easy—for Yourself!

1. Have the room completely ready for fingerpainting before it is time for the art lesson. Have all materials distributed and ready for an orderly beginning of the lesson.

2. Overlap at least two layers of newspaper on all working areas so that no paint or water will get on the desks or tables.

3. Be sure each child has an old shirt on backwards. A string or cotton roving tied around the waist holds the shirt close to the body and prevents it from getting in the way when leaning over.

4. Have at least two small cans for water. If more than three or four children are in the group, you may want an extra can.

5. Arrange the room as you would for a tempera painting lesson: four desks pushed together make a good table area, three children in a group with the fourth desk used for supplies.

6. If chairs and desks are separate, move all the chairs to one side of the room. This will keep them clean, make it easier to paint, and provide a space where the children may sit when they have finished painting. It will make the lesson and the clean-up orderly. If the chairs are attached to the desks, have the children stand in back of the chairs to paint, and remain standing until all the clean-up is finished.

7. Always stand to fingerpaint.

8. Be sure children paint on the shiny side of the paper.

9. Have a paper towel at each person's painting area. Have him put it under the newspaper so that he can slide it out easily at clean-up time. Let each child put his own paper towel under the newspaper so that he knows exactly where it is when he needs it.

10. Yellow makes less contrast on the white paper than other colors do, so you may want to eliminate it if using only one color on a paper. It is fine if blended with a second color.

11. Avoid "erasing" a design more than a couple of times as too many "erasures" lessen the color contrast in the painting.

12. Swing a motion to the top—or off the top—of the paper for the beginning of the design. Gradually lower the height of the design as additional parts are added.

13. If the paper tends to move as you are working on it, lift one edge and put a *little* water under it. That will hold the paper in place.

Variations

1. Blend two or three colors together, blending them in specific areas only so as to produce a more varied and interesting color effect.

2. Use a piece of cardboard or the edge of a tongue depressor instead of your hand to make the design. A sharper imprint, both in line and color shading, will result.

3. Make a monoprint from the original fingerpainting. A monoprint is made by laying another paper—manila, white drawing, or colored construction—over the wet fingerpainting. Rub your hand over the back of the paper that is being printed, then peel it off the original painting. The monoprint will have a different texture from the original painting.

4. Prepare a paper for fingerpainting (water and paint). Immediately lay another paper over it as if making a monoprint. Use a tongue depressor, blunt or pointed pencil, or any similar tool (or combination of them) to rub onto the back of the paper being printed. Make the same type of unit abstract design as you would for a fingerpainting. Pull the two papers apart. The result will be similar to a monoprint.

Variations for Lower Grades

1. Use the same type of rhythmic repeat motions as in previous fingerpainting. Make the first one all across the top of the paper. Change the type of motion and repeat a little lower down, so that it slightly overlaps the bottom of the top row. Continue down the paper, each row with a different motion and each one different from the one above.

2. Make a monoprint of a painting like the one described above. This is done by laying a piece of any kind of paper over the wet fingerpainting and rubbing the back of the paper with the palm of the hand. Immediately pull the two papers apart.

OBJECTIVES

1. **To use fingerpainting skills for realistic composition.**
2. **To show the versatility of fingerpaint.**
3. **To stimulate creative growth in a familiar medium.**

(For grades 4 through 6)

Lesson Three: Not Just Therapy!

REALISTIC FINGERPAINTED PICTURES

In this age of the psychiatrist, fingerpainting has often been relegated to the realm of therapy. It is sometimes considered only as a means of giving vent to pent up childhood emotions. Not so! Fingerpainting can be a wonderful medium in which creative and well-designed pictures can be achieved.

In early childhood, fingerpainting often represents the means for a one finger picture of a house, a tree, and a flower. To show the versatility of this fluid medium, the child is then exposed to non-objective, rhythm designs and the child finds this a mistake-free, easy and enjoyable pastime, forgetting he once could make a picture. It is now time to let him try the many techniques he employed in his designing in a realistic composition.

He has now learned that by using more than one finger he can achieve a great deal of interesting and varied patterns in his finger-

60

painting. His palm, his fist, the side of his hand, are now ready to develop a picture of reality and significance. The subject matter can be anything he chooses, from an underwater scene to cowboys and Indians. The problem is to create a picture without using the one-finger method.

With a little practice, the student can see how effectively he can make a tree by using the side of his hand for the trunk with fingertip leaves, a flat palm could produce a river or lake, his knuckles could suggest far-off trees or rocks.

If time permits, experiments should be tried before the actual composition is made. On a first sheet of fingerpaint paper, have the class make one realistic object at a time, erasing each one, and continuing to another and another. When the paper begins to dry, it is time to begin again, this time composing a realistic picture utilizing the objects made during the experiments. Caution the class to beware of trying to put too much into a picture and to avoid the use of minute details. These pictures should be done freely and on a large scale, with as much imagination and exaggeration as possible.

Remember—fingerpainting need not only be a means of emotional release, but it may result also in a creative and artistic expression.

Make It Easy—for Yourself!

1. Overlap at least two layers of newspaper on all working areas so that no paint or water will get on the desks or tables.
2. Be sure each person has an old shirt on backwards. A piece of string (or cotton roving) tied around the waist holds the shirt close to the body and makes it easier to work, especially when leaning over.
3. Arrange the room as you would for a tempera painting lesson: four desks pushed together make a good table area, three children in a group with the fourth desk used for supplies.
4. Have at least two small cans for water for each group. If more than three or four children are in the group you may want an extra can.
5. Be sure children paint on the shiny side of the paper.
6. Have the room completely ready before the beginning of

the lesson. Have a paper towel at each person's painting area. Have him put it under the newspaper so that he can slide it out easily at clean-up time. (Let him put it under the newspaper so he knows exactly where it is when needed.)

7. Yellow makes less contrast on the paper than other colors, so you may want to eliminate it if using only one color for a painting.

8. If chairs and desks are separate, move all the chairs to one side of the room. This will keep them clean, make it easier to paint, and leave a place where the children may sit when they have finished painting, making it easier to keep the lesson and the clean-up orderly. If the chairs are attached to the desks, have the children stand in back of the chairs to paint, and remain standing until all clean-up is finished.

9. Always stand to fingerpaint.

10. If the paper tends to move while you are working on it, lift one edge and put a *little* water under it. That will hold the paper in place.

OBJECTIVES

1. To introduce multicolor design in fingerpainting.

2. To stimulate imagination in nonobjective design by of-
fering a new experience.

3. To combine the beauty of line with the excitement of
color.

4. To have further direct experience in a fluid medium.

(For grades 4 through 6)

Lesson Four: Are You Ready?

FINGERPAINTING WITH PRIMARY COLORS

ARE YOU READY FOR A CHALLENGE? WELL, HERE'S
a lesson that combines imagination and skill for both
the teacher and student.

Now that you're an expert on fingerpainting, go a
step beyond the ordinary and try combining the three
primary colors in one picture. The results are worth the
effort and by following our basic fingerpainting techniques you will find it quite easy to manage.

The best motivation for such a visual medium is a teacher demonstration which will bring forth "oohs" and "ahs" as the paint blends
and mixes and forms new colors. For the first try, keep compositions
non-objective in design. Start by placing the three scoops of colors

63

fairly near to one another in any area of the paper. You may begin in a corner, toward the center or at the bottom or top of your paper. Spread out the colors one by one until the paper is covered. Then by using your hand as a tool begin pushing the pigment around until it starts to overlap and mix and form new colors.

You are now combining line design with color. Keep your lines flowing and simple and rhythmic in nature. Starting at the point where color was first applied, radiate out in all directions. Keep the design simple and work only until the secondary colors—orange, green, and violet—appear. If this design is overworked, the colors will become muddy and unattractive. Keep it fast and simple.

If enough jars are available, have the class work in groups sharing the primary colors. If you must pass out the colors, have each child mark the spot on which he wants his color. This could be done with pencil when the paper is still dry. The jars are small enough to fit on a tray and can be carried in this manner from child to child. Don't try to serve the whole class at once with water and paint because the paper may dry too quickly. Instead work the class in small sections or rows.

You and your class will enjoy this exciting visual experience and marvel at the colorful and unique results.

Make It Easy—for Yourself!

1. Overlap at least two layers of newspaper on all work areas so that no paint or water will get on the desks or tables.
2. Be sure each person has an old shirt on backwards. A piece of string (or cotton roving) tied around the waist holds the shirt close to the body and makes it easier to work, especially when leaning over.
3. Arrange the room as you would for a tempera painting lesson: four desks pushed together make a good table area, three children in a group with the fourth desk used for supplies.
4. Have at least two small cans for water for each group. If more than three or four children are in the group, you may want an extra can.
5. Be sure children paint on the shiny side of the paper.
6. Have the room completely ready before the beginning of the lesson. Have a paper towel at each person's paint-

ing area. Have him put it under the newspaper so that he can slide it out easily at clean-up time. (Let him put it under the newspaper so he knows exactly where it is when needed.)

7. If chairs and desks are separate, move all the chairs to one side of the room. This will keep them clean, make it easier to paint, and leave a place where the children may sit when they have finished painting, and will therefore make it easier to keep the lesson and the clean-up orderly. If the chairs are attached to the desks, have the children stand in back of the chairs to paint, and remain standing until all clean-up is finished.

8. Always stand to fingerpaint.

9. If the paper tends to move while you are working on it, lift one edge and put a *little* water under it. That will hold the paper in place.

10. Every child should have a damp sponge, cloth, paper towel, or piece of cotton batting with which he may clean his hands between colors. This will be helpful for better control of color.

Variations

1. Pass out the three colors on a small piece of paper to each child. In any way he wants, he may then use the colors to make a realistic picture, mixing and blending the colors on the wet fingerpaint paper, very much like a painter working from a palette.

2. Have each child cover the paper with one color and form a design or picture by adding the other two on top. This must be done quickly for good results and can not be overworked. More experience and skill is needed for this variation.

Lesson Five: You Must Have Sunshine

FINGERPAINTED BLUEPRINTS

WHEN AN ADMIRING THOUGH SKEPTICAL VIEWER comments, "You don't mean that your class made those?" you proudly reply, "Of course, they're fingerpainted blueprints." You've never heard of fingerpainted blueprints! Well, now, let's do something about that!

To begin with, make sure the weather cooperates with you, for you must have sunshine in order to make blueprints. When the right day arrives make the same careful preparations that you always do for fingerpainting. You'll need the usual newspaper, shirts, paper towel, fingerpaint, and cans of water. No, I didn't forget fingerpaint paper—you won't need it this time. Instead you will need pieces of glass about 9 x 12 with all the edges taped as a precaution. In addition you'll need some extra materials for the blueprinting part of the process: blueprint paper, water, sponges, and more newspaper.

Some people think you can fingerpaint only on a special kind of paper, but that isn't so. You can fingerpaint on almost anything, and today we're going to do it on glass. So begin by pouring a little water onto the glass—just a little, though, as the glass can't absorb it the way paper would. Spread the water over the whole area, then scoop up about a tablespoonful of fingerpaint. Lay it on the center of the glass, stir it with the hand flat, then quickly spread it over all of the glass. Have a rather thick layer of paint.

Have the class gathered about you as you continue your demonstration. What kind of fingerpainting will you make? Any kind: a simple rhythmic repeat pattern, an abstract, a more realistic picture— any kind that looks good and has a feeling of motion to it. So, with a flowing line move your hand from the bottom of the glass all the way to the top. See what happened? All the paint was pushed off the glass in some places and was piled up thicker in other places. Try it again—almost to the top. Use your hand in a different way this time, making a pleasing grouping of motions and lines. The painting is small, so complete it quickly, adding only a finishing touch here or there.

Pretty, isn't it! See how the glass shows in some places where all or most of the paint was pushed away. But look how it's piled thick in other places. Make a nice picture, wouldn't it? But we don't have glass enough for everyone, and anyway it would break if you dropped it. So———

So, let's blueprint it! That's right, blueprint it. While this is drying, let's look at the blueprint paper and see what we do with it.

Pull a sheet of blueprint paper from the end of the package, being careful not to expose the rest in the package. One side of the paper is white and looks just like any other paper, but the other side is very special. See, it's a rather grey blue. That's because it is covered with two chemicals that just lay on top of each other. They don't mix together, in fact they both come right off if any water gets on them. If I just touch them with a wet finger—like that—see what happened. A white spot where the chemicals came off. But if I put the paper in the sunlight for a little while something else will happen. Sun combines the two chemicals and also adheres them to the paper. The length of exposure to the sun will have to be determined by experimentation, as the sun's strength will vary from day to day. On a bright day begin by exposing it for about 15 seconds. Then try increasing or decreasing the time of exposure until a bright blue results.

To demonstrate how the light prints an object, lay a pair of scissors or any other object that's handy, on the blue print paper. After the paper has been exposed to the sun for the correct length of time, hold it under running water or slosh it back and forth in a pail of water. Hold it upright for a few moments to allow the extra water to drain off.

A surprise, isn't it? Where it was covered by the pair of scissors all the chemicals washed off and the paper is white—a blueprint of the scissors! Where the sunlight touched the blueprint paper it is now a lovely blue, much prettier than it was before. But there's that white spot where I put my wet finger! (Make sure that spot was in the area exposed to the sunlight so that there will be proof of the damage of getting unexposed blueprint paper wet.)

What would happen if I took another sheet of blueprint paper and placed my fingerpainting over it instead of a pair of scissors? Sure, it would blueprint the fingerpainting instead of the scissors. Where there isn't any paint the sun can get through the glass and turn the paper—— blue, that's right! And where the fingerpaint is piled up so thick that no sun can get through, nothing will happen to the chemicals, so they will —— right, wash off and leave the paper white.

Place a fresh piece of blueprint paper on a heavy piece of cardboard to act as a tray, place the fingerpainted glass on top of the blueprint paper. Carefully carry it to the sunlight and expose it for the proper length of time. Place the blueprint paper under running water (or in a pail) and right before your eyes appears your fingerpainting— as a blueprint. Magic, isn't it? But beautiful magic that's lots of fun. Place the wet (but drained) blueprint between sheets of newspaper to dry.

Now that the "ohs" and "ahs" have died down, divide the class into groups. Proceed with the fingerpainting and then with the blueprinting. Have assistants for various responsibilities so that the whole lesson will continue smoothly. Extra pails of water should be available so that when a blueprint is finished an assistant can wash and dry the glass to have it ready for another person to use.

If you can wait until the blueprints are dry (that's hard to do!), you'll find that they have become a slightly brighter blue than when they were wet. Mat or mount them on white paper and find a space to display every one of them. They'll all deserve an honored spot—

and you won't be able to keep your eyes off of them any more than anyone else will!

Make It Easy—for Yourself!

1. Be sure it is a sunny day when you do fingerpainted blueprints. Sun develops the print, so the brighter the day the better the results. Light for blueprinting is better in spring and early fall than during the winter months.
2. Cover all work areas with newspaper.
3. Have several pieces of glass about 9 x 12. Tape all edges of the glass with masking or other adhesive tape for protection against cuts.
4. Have several sponges to use to wash the glass after the fingerpainting has been made. If there is no sink in the classroom, have a pail of water to wash off the fingerpaint.
5. Be sure each person has an old shirt on backwards to protect clothing.
6. Have a small can of water for each group.
7. Have a paper towel at each person's painting area.
8. Have a jar of fingerpaint for each group. Any color will do as the color used makes absolutely no difference in the blueprint that results.
9. If chairs and desks are separate, remove chairs to the side of the room. If the chairs are attached to the desks, have the children stand in back of the desks to paint—and remain standing until all the clean-up is finished.
10. Have the children experiment with several positions of the hand and several motions before beginning the final painting.
11. Always stand to fingerpaint.
12. Handle all blueprint paper yourself—or make it the responsibility of just one person. Blueprint paper is developed by sunlight, so avoid exposure to the light until ready to print. Open the package at one end only and remove each sheet as it is needed. Be sure your hands are dry whenever you touch undeveloped blueprint paper as water removes the chemicals from it.
13. For each piece of glass, have a piece of cardboard as large

or slightly larger. This is a firm base on which to lay the blueprint paper and glass so as to make them easier to handle.

14. On the day you are going to blueprint, experiment ahead of time so that you will know how many seconds to expose the blueprint. This depends upon how strong the sunlight is, and might vary from only ten or twelve seconds to as many as ninety or even more.

15. If there is no sink in the room, have a large pan or pail of water in which to wash the blueprint paper after exposure. Be sure to get off all the undeveloped chemicals as they will stain the paper if allowed to remain.

16. It will be easier not to have everyone in the class fingerpainting and blueprinting at the same time. Appoint various helpers: timekeepers, someone to give out blueprint paper as needed, someone to see that blueprints are placed in newspaper for drying, two children to wash and carefully dry the glass after each fingerpainting. Divide the rest of the class into pairs to take turns fingerpainting and blueprinting.

17. Have pieces of newspaper torn in half or quarters so that wet blueprints can be placed between them to dry and be piled one on top of another. Place only six or eight in each pile so that they can dry.

Variations

1. Blueprint a combination of cut paper and fingerpainted pictures. Plan a picture—cut part of it from paper and lay it on the blueprint paper. Fingerpaint (on glass) the rest of the picture. Continue to blueprint as previously described. For example: cut a jungle animal from paper. On the piece of glass blueprint sweeping lines to give the impression of jungle foliage. Blueprint in the regular way.

2. Use dried materials to blueprint. Make an interesting arrangement on blueprint paper of dried and pressed grasses, ferns, leaves. Place a piece of plain glass over it to keep materials from moving and blueprint in the regular way.

3. Use other real materials to blueprint. Arrange related materials on blueprint paper and print. For example: arrange materials associated with sewing—needle and thread, scissors, buttons.

Variations for Lower Grades

1. Fold a piece of light-weight paper in half two or three times (depending upon the thickness of the paper). Cut through the several layers at one time to make an interesting design pattern. Open the cut paper and lay it on a piece of blueprint paper. A piece of glass over it will help to hold it flat but is not necessary. Blueprint it in the usual way.

2. Cut a piece of paper (any scrap paper will do) into many small pieces. Drop a few onto a piece of blueprint paper. As it is exposed to the sunlight, gradually drop the remaining scraps over the blueprint paper. Continue the blueprint process in the usual way. The resulting print will be a picture with variations of blues and white.

WAX CRAYON

CHAPTER **4**

Wax Crayon

Lesson One: When Is a Circle Not a Circle?

BEGIN WITH A CIRCLE

WHEN IS A CIRCLE NOT A CIRCLE? WHY, WHEN IT'S a clock, or a yo-yo, or a face. A flat paper circle doesn't have to stay that way, you know—so let's change it.

Take a piece of colored construction paper and begin cutting a circle from it. Make it about four or five inches across. As soon as you have started cutting ask your class what they think it is going to be. Of course they have no way of knowing, so you'll get all kinds of answers. Perhaps someone says a boat. No, it isn't that. A rabbit? No, not that either. But by now you've nearly finished, so at least one person says it's a circle. Yes, that's right—and you hold it up.

74

But it could be something else. What else looks something like a circle?

Someone may suggest the clock. Of course it could be a clock. All I'd have to do would be put numbers on it and the hands and I'd have a clock. What else could it be? What else in this room could start as a circle? The globe—the ball we play with—the glasses you have on—good, even a person's face could start as a circle. We'd have to add eyes and ears and nose and mouth—and hair, too.

Have the children name as many things as possible from the classroom that begin as a circle, then ask them to think of things at home that could be made from a circle. Such things as cups and saucers, lamps, tables and pans will be suggested. Comment about each one of them. Then—what would you find outdoors that we could begin as a circle? Of course, the wheel on your father's car, or the wheel on your bicycle or your toy truck. Or perhaps it will be a stop sign, or a street light, or many, many other things.

Now it's time to stop thinking of all the things it *might* be and make it into one *real* thing. Give out pieces of 12 x 18 manila paper and smaller pieces of colored construction paper. A pair of scissors, a tiny bit of paste, and a box of crayons are all the other materials necessary.

Urge each child to do his own thinking. What is his circle going to become? Don't worry about the size or color of the circle. It can become a golf ball or the wheel of a diesel truck just as well. Paste it on the construction paper and add parts to it if you like. Make it into a clown's face, or a wheel on a toy wagon, or an ice cream cone, or a kitchen table—or whatever your circle is going to be. There's lots of paper left, so use your crayons to finish your picture. Fill all the paper so that your crayons and your circle tell a story.

When the pictures are finished, talk about them—then display them. You'll be surprised how many things begin with a circle that don't have to stay a circle.

Make It Easy—for Yourself!

1. Have circles already drawn on colored construction paper, if you like. The important thing is not cutting a circle, but using lots of imagination to make something out of it.

2. As you walk about the room during the lesson, collect the scissors, paste, and scraps of paper as soon as the circles are cut and pasted. This will permit more work space at the children's desks and eliminate the need for clean-up at the end of the lesson.

Variations

1. Use a square or a rectangle as the beginning shape.
2. Make the whole picture with crayons. Begin some part of it as a circle (or square or rectangle).

Lesson Two: Spring Fever

DRAWING OUTDOORS

LET'S TAKE ADVANTAGE OF A WARM, SUNNY DAY. The weather is far too pleasant for us to stay indoors, even for an art lesson. We have spring fever. So gather materials together and let's go outside.

Begin the lesson in the classroom by telling the class what they are going to do. Tell them that sometimes artists like to draw exactly what they see. Then look out the classroom windows. Notice that you don't see everything at one time—that you have to move your eyes from place to place to see it all. Each time you move your eyes you are seeing a new picture.

77

Then learn to plan—to "find"—a picture. Point, with arm extended straight out, at the imaginary edges of a picture—as though you were tracing the four edges of a piece of paper. Everything inside will be your picture. Go over the edges several times: see what comes to and even off the top of the "paper"; see what goes to the bottom and off the bottom edge; see what comes to each side, and off each side edge. Look carefully to see what is included in the picture, and where each thing is.

Tell the class that when they go outside, each one of them will "find" his own picture by drawing out the edges of his "paper" (in the air, that is) just as he has done in the classroom while looking out the windows.

Pass out crayons, boxes of twenty-four colors if you have them or can borrow them for the occasion from an upper grade. Look at the variety of colors—the several shades of green, for example. Then look at the trees or grass you can see from the windows. Do all the greens look the same? Do some of them seem to have more yellow in them? Which green crayon would be good for that part? And is there any dark green in the trees? How could you make it look like that? Talk about the variety of some of the other colors in the box and where they might be used. Make it important that the children see the colors as they really look as well as the sizes and shapes of things.

Let the class feel really professional by showing them a way to hold a drawing board—a piece of heavy cardboard to which you have taped a piece of manila paper approximately 12 x 18. With one hand at the top of the drawing board, hold it facing away from you. Then turn your arm so that the drawing board faces toward you, your arm in back of it and your fingers toward you. At the same time let the lower corner of the board come to rest on your hip. You will find it is an easy position to hold and it will free all the work area for drawing. Let each child try holding a drawing board as you pass them out to the class. Even children as young as first or second graders will be able to handle it and will get a sense of achievement from having learned something they will think is adult.

Now you're outside. Let each child choose a spot within a large area that you have designated for them. Encourage them to look in all directions for an interesting picture. Then let each child "find" his picture as he did in the classroom by drawing the edges of the "paper" in the air. Some children will want to stand to draw, others will sit with the drawing boards on the grass or in their laps. Just be comfortable so that you can concentrate on seeing and drawing it on paper with crayons.

You will want to move about your class quickly, stopping for a moment to encourage and help each child. "That's a good beginning. Glad you noticed that the tree came all the way off the top of the picture." Or, "Did you notice the color of the mountain? Does it all look the same?" Encourage each child to see for himself. If he is putting in the little details that are sometimes overlooked, comment about it to show your appreciation. If he hasn't noticed them, ask a question that will help to bring them to his attention. Above all, make it a vital experience that will be worth repeating.

When the children have returned to the classroom, let them remove the tape to take their pictures off the drawing boards. Have a few moments of sharing time so that each child will see what all the others have done. Then display all, or as many as possible of them, perhaps grouping together scenes that are of the same areas.

Make It Easy—for Yourself!

1. Use a papercutter to cut a piece of heavy cardboard for each child to use as a drawing board. Make it a little larger than 12 x 18—the size can vary slightly to suit the cardboard available.

2. Use 12 x 18 manila paper, or cut it to a *slightly* smaller size.

3. Tape the paper to the drawing board. A piece of masking tape on two sides of the paper is fine.

4. Carry the drawing board (with paper attached) as a tray. The box of crayons can be held on top of the "tray" under the thumb of one hand. That way nothing will spill.

5. See that each child finds a spot to work that is away from everyone else. ("Artists don't like to be bothered when they're working.")

6. No pencils. Let the crayons do all the drawing.

7. Of course, the youngest children will draw things as they see them—not as an adult sees them. They will continue to make the same kind of figures they always make, and they will still make the sky just a line across the top of the paper.

Variation for Grades K through 3

Use tempera paint instead of crayons. Let four children work in a group, one egg carton for paints for each group and one jar of water for each group.

Variations for Grades 4 through 6

1. Use different media: charcoal, chalk, pencils, watercolors.
2. Pick out only one object and make a close-up of it, trying to observe and reproduce as many of the details as possible. (For example: one unusual tree; the bicycle rack; the slide or jungle gym.)
3. Try to recreate the mood of a scene without reproducing it as it appears. (For example: the noise—or loneliness— of a crowded area; the quietness of an open area with a clump of trees; the confusion at a construction site.)

OBJECTIVES

1. **To encourage the use of mixed color with crayon.**

2. **To give a basic introduction of primary and secondary colors to young children.**

3. **To show a wider range for the use of crayon.**

4. **To experiment with colors and to see their effects upon each other.**

   (For grades 1 through 6)

Lesson Three: Color It Creative

BLENDING WAX CRAYONS

HERE IS A TREE: COLOR IT GREEN. HERE IS A HOUSE: color it red. This type of crayon art is not only stifling but also dangerous to the young and eager mind. Here is a box of crayons and a piece of paper and that's all you need for wonderful, creative, and meaningful artistic adventures. Color it—creative!

Aside from the many realistic forms of artistic crayon drawings, this wax medium can also be used as a tool for learning and experimenting with color. Everyone knows you can mix paint to achieve a new color or hue, but how many people realize that it can also be done with crayons? Why let your children be satisfied with the ready-made colors straight out of the box? They

81

can make new colors which will add a unique quality to their drawings.

One of the best ways to learn about making new colors is to use red, yellow, and blue—the primary colors. When these are combined they make violet, orange, and green—the secondary colors. This is particularly fascinating to young children as they see these transformations appear before their eyes.

Have each child make a wide band of each of the primary colors across his white drawing paper. Divide each band of color approximately into thirds and on the last two sections add each of the other two primary colors. For example, on the yellow band apply blue on the second section and red on the last section. You will then see yellow, green, and orange on the yellow band; red, orange, and violet on the red band; and blue, green, and violet on the blue band. You now have the three primary colors and the three secondary colors. Let's use them.

These areas of colors may be cut in many various ways to form realistic or abstract pictures. Let us consider an abstract composition using our primary and secondary colors.

First cut out free-form shapes, one of each color. Try arranging them on a 12 x 18 piece of white or colored paper. Decide how many shapes you want to use and discard the others. Choice depends mainly on your own color preference. To relieve any monotony of too much crayon, a few shapes of colored construction paper may be added. Let the construction paper shapes follow the contours of the crayon areas.

You will find that these arrangements are visually attractive, in that each one is different and unique—and creative!

Make It Easy—for Yourself!

1. Have the class select only their three primary color crayons and put the others away.
2. If the paper is peeled from the crayons so that the side of the crayon can be used, the areas will be covered quickly and smoothly.
3. When the crayon work is nearly completed, pass out other materials (scissors, paste, 12 x 18 background paper).

This will avoid crowding the work area but still provide materials as they are needed.

4. As children finish with various materials—for example, scissors—the teacher may collect them. This provides increased work area and a more orderly clean-up.

Variations

1. Use any colors to create either an abstract or realistic picture with this blending technique.
2. Create a blended abstract directly on the paper, eliminating the cutting and pasting.
3. Use liquid media to achieve the blending of new colors in either abstract or realistic pictures.

OBJECTIVES

1. **To use crayon in a different way from the regular line technique.**

2. **To demonstrate the blending of primary colors to create new colors.**

3. **To create a rhythmic picture by repeating a single motif.**

4. **To be able to make a pleasing arrangement through the grouping of a repeated motif.**

(For grades 3 through 6)

Lesson Four: Magic, It Is!

RUBBED CRAYON PICTURES

How about being a magician for a change! Even without saying "abracadabra" you can make a picture appear just by rubbing a crayon across a piece of paper. Magic, it is!

What would you like to have appear by magic? A clown, a sailboat, a tree, a man, a flower, a house, a rabbit? Whatever it is, cut it out of oaktag or any heavy piece of paper (approximately 5 x 7 inches). Be sure your object looks good as a solid shape, that it doesn't need any extra lines drawn on it to complete it.

In the meantime have cut some long pieces of newsprint—easel paper, that is. Cut the regular size 18 x 24 paper in half so that it is 9 x 24. Also peel the wrappers from four crayons: black, red, yellow, and blue.

Now for the magic, black magic, at that! Hide the sailboat or clown or whatever you cut out underneath the long piece of newsprint. Lay the black crayon flat on the plain piece of newsprint—over the place where the picture has been hidden. Gently press against the crayon, stroking the flat side out in all directions. Out of no place the object appears on your paper. See, there it is! You are a magician! Don't worry about the extra bits of black area that appear outside the man, or the house, or the rabbit. Move the object that is under the paper. Be a magician again. See, there is the second clown, or tree, or flower.

Move it again and again, adjusting the space each time to make a pleasing arrangement. Sometimes let two men or two trees overlap as though one was in back of the other. Or leave a wide space between. Make a group of others close together. Just make an interesting arrangement. A magician can certainly do that!

When the paper is nicely filled—but not crowded—use the other three crayons to fill in the background. Use the crayons flat, of course, and first be sure to remove the shape from underneath. Today we're using the primary colors—red, yellow, and blue—so that we can see the new colors they make when they mix together. Let's start with the blue. With the crayon flat, rub a large area until a big blue section appears. Immediately make another blue section the same way, but this time make it a different size and shape. Looks prettier already, doesn't it!

But let's get on to the yellow. Make two or three yellow areas in different parts of the picture—the crayon flat, of course. We don't want any lines from the crayon, just smooth yellow areas of color. There, that's good! Let the yellow overlap some of the blue. See, where the two colors mixed you have green. Now let's finish the picture by filling in all the rest of the paper with the last color. Keep the red crayon flat. Let it mix with the blue and the yellow. Purple and orange appear. There's magic in the color, too.

Looks good, doesn't it! Now how about giving them names. Every good picture deserves a good name. Maybe "Sailboat Race in the Sunset" or "Trees in a Lighted Sky." But they're your pictures, so you think of a name. Be sure to display the results, too. There'll even be magic in the comments you hear about them!

Make It Easy—for Yourself!

1. Have the paper cut the right size: small pieces of oaktag about 5 x 7, and long pieces of easel paper, 9 x 24.
2. No pencil drawing first! Use the black crayon if any preliminary drawing is desired. Draw only on one side of the paper, making any changes in size or shape without trying to erase. The lines will not make any difference in the result.
3. Before using the cut-out shape, turn it over to the plain side. Does it look the way you want it to? Does the shape show what it really is?
4. Put away all the crayons except the black and the primary colors to avoid their use.

Variations

1. Use the same technique but cut several simple geometric shapes: circles, squares, diamonds, triangles.
2. Use seasonal or holiday motifs for the "magic" shape.
3. Use chalk or a combination of crayon and chalk.
4. Use a variety of colors in place of the primary colors—or another color in place of black.

OBJECTIVES

1. To introduce the *crayon resist* technique.

2. To encourage imagination by using common media in an unusual technique.

3. To correlate background colors and the mood of a picture.

(For grades K through 6)

Lesson Five: Running Wild

CRAYON RESIST

LET IMAGINATIONS RUN WILD! ROCKETS COMING out of the blue; monsters in the black of night; dinosaurs in the mist of grey; happy faces glowing in the warmth of red are just a few ideas for an effective art lesson.

Often we get bogged down or bored when we have used an art medium or technique over and over again. It may be an excellent art lesson, but the excitement somehow is gone. It's time for a shot in the arm!

For example, let's talk about "crayon resist." Children of all ages are thrilled when they make a crayon drawing and then cover it with paint and discover that their picture still mysteriously appears as the wax crayon *resists* the water base paint. It is not enough, however, to have your class make any kind of a picture and just paint over it. For such a special technique we need special excitement and motivation.

Let's try making an imaginary monster peering out at us from the grey mist of pre-historic times. Draw in the monster—make him big, bright, and unique. Heavily applied crayon will stand out, and the colors will seem to sing. Then add background to complete the setting. Use your crayons heavily and combine many colors. Next choose a paint color which fits the mood of your picture. For our make-believe creature, let's choose a misty grey which suggests the gloom and fog of some long past era. Slowly paint over the crayon drawing. Some of the paint will catch on our crayon, making our monster appear to be actually engulfed in the mist. Remember, the background color is very important for setting the tone or mood of our picture and should be chosen carefully.

Make this a special picture—use your crayons heavily, use lots of bright colors, keep the picture simple and big. Contrast the background color with the crayon drawing. Don't make something ordinary—let your imagination run wild!

Make It Easy—for Yourself!

1. Have several separate painting areas, each covered with newspaper.
2. Offer as many colors as possible for the painted background.
3. Have the class take turns painting as they finish their crayon drawings.
4. Have an area set up for drying the pictures. Cover the area with newspapers so the wet paintings will not touch anything else.
5. No pencils—draw with crayon.

Variations

1. Use bright colors to make an abstract design. Leave blank paper around it so that when it is painted the design will seem to float.
2. Use holiday motifs for the crayon work. Use suitable background colors.

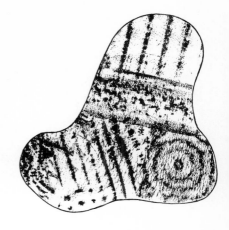
Lesson Six: Rub-a-Dub-Dub

CRAYON RUBBING FOR TEXTURE

"RUB-A-DUB-DUB, THREE MEN IN A TUB," MAY well be the expression to describe this lesson. In many Asian countries, rubbings of *bas relief* carvings are sold to tourists, as they have a highly decorative and unique quality. You have probably used this same technique as a child, rubbing over a penny with pencil and paper to reproduce Lincoln's image. This technique is the basis for an informative art lesson.

Texture is important to an artist if he is to create realistic and meaningful works of art. Unfortunately, texture or surface feeling is often ignored in the art education of the young child. A tree is brown, bricks are red, and everything has a one-tone flat appearance in most children's art work—and thinking. It is time to introduce texture.

First discuss texture, the way things feel. Compare a rough and a smooth surface in the room. Have the class become aware of how things feel as well as how they look. Next take a piece of 9 x 12 white paper and a crayon and ask the class how a surface texture can be reproduced on paper. Then illustrate it to them by placing the paper on a rough surface and rubbing over it with the crayon. They will see how the raised parts of the surface take on color while the recessed parts remain white. Have each student explore the room to see how many textures and patterns he can find. Make sure that enough paper is available for each child to have large areas of different colored textures. Remember that cracks, rows of books, and grill work make wonderful patterns.

Now we must use the technique for a finished product. One way is to have each child create a cut-out picture using the different colored textures he has made. For example, cutting out the textures in the form of clothing can lead to an exciting figure with perhaps a plaid shirt made from rubbing a screen, corduroy trousers from rubbing crayons lined up in a box, or curly hair from a cement rubbing. Any kind of a picture can be created, preferably on a 12 x 18 colored paper background.

This lesson is not only informative but delightful for the child who is allowed to release his exploring instinct. Rub-a-dub-dub!

Make It Easy—for Yourself!

1. Keep a tight rein on the class during the exploring period. So much activity need not lead to chaos.
2. In order to discover a wide range of textures, caution the class not to discuss where each has been discovered.
3. Be sure to point out that rubbings can be done on anything—books lined up on a shelf, openings on a desk, crayons in a box.
4. This is an excellent way to use old crayons which can be peeled and used on their sides for a smooth, even effect.
5. Limit to two or three the number of crayons to be carried around the room.

Variations

1. Use only one texture in a picture, completing it with cut paper, paint, or any other media.
2. Combine different textures to form a design.
3. Make a rubbing of many objects at home and outdoors. Combine them in a *collage*.

Variations for Higher Grades

1. Use an india ink or diluted paint wash to highlight the crayon rubbing.
2. Cut out a shape from black paper using a realistic motif. Use the resulting frame (negative stencil) mounted on the crayon work which will then become a bright textured picture.
3. Make a realistic picture. Instead of drawing the picture, rub each of the parts over one or several textures or patterns.

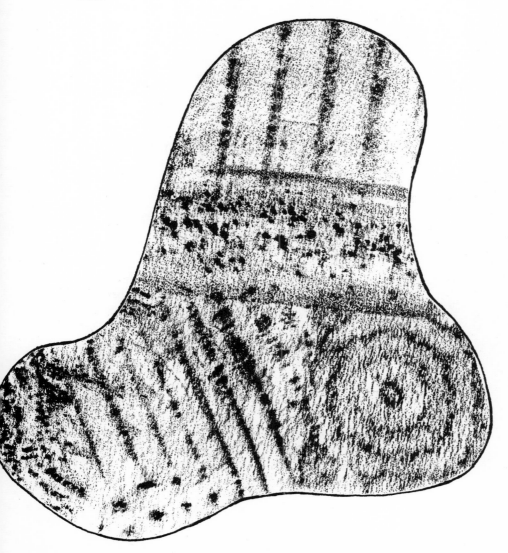

Lesson Seven: What Is It?

ABSTRACTING A FORM

WHAT IS IT? WHAT DOES IT MEAN? THESE ARE often the questions following the viewing of abstract and non-objective art, commonly lumped together in the vague term of "modern art." Here is a lesson for young children designed to give them a basic understanding in creating an abstract design.

Begin by placing simple-shaped objects such as bottles and vases around the room. Talk to the class about how these shapes look. Are they made of curves or straight lines—or a combination of both? Do they look flat, or do they look round? Why do they look round? The light makes them look that way, doesn't it? Which part of the object is lightest? That's right, the part closest to the light. And see how dark the other side looks where it's in the shadow.

Then have the class use crayon to draw these objects on a piece of 9 x 12 manila paper. When a satisfactory drawing has been made, it should then be colored, the emphasis on making it appear rounded. This is done by shading. The outside edges of the object should be colored very dark, gradually fading out the color toward the source of light. The dark colors will seem to recede while the lighter tones appear to come forward, giving a rounded or three-dimensional look to the object.

When the drawing is completed, it should then be cut out, and, with a black or dark crayon, traced on another piece of 9 x 12 paper. The cut-out is then moved and retraced over all of the paper until the entire sheet is divided into small areas created by overlapping and tracing the cut-out.

The next step is to add color to the over-all design. Limit it to three crayons and have the class color in their designs, one shape at a time. Color variations may be achieved by overlapping and by varying the pressure for light and dark. When this has been finished, have the class go over the black outline shapes to sharpen the image of the design.

There will appear in each design the original drawing, but it will be divided into numerous areas. It will, however, retain its former unified shape and outline. Thus, there is achieved an abstract design with meaning. One can more easily understand the abstractions of Picasso and other famous masters after this lesson.

For display purposes, both the abstract and the original drawing can be mounted on 12 x 18 paper. This will clearly indicate to viewers the meaning and relationship of the abstract design to the original object.

Make It Easy—for Yourself!

1. Cover work areas with large newsprint or newspaper, as the crayon will go to the edge of the design.
2. Pass out both sheets of paper, scissors, and crayons at the beginning so students may work at their own speed.
3. Collect the scraps before the design is attempted. This will provide a greater work area.
4. Collect scissors or have them put away as soon as each child has cut out his shape. This means there will be little clean-up to do—only the newspapers.

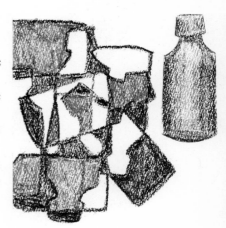

Variations for Higher Grades

1. Follow the same procedure, but instead of cutting out the entire shape and tracing it, use only various lines in the shape to form a design. For example: dissect the lines of the shape and overlap them to create areas. Continue until the paper is once again divided into interesting shapes which then can be colored.
2. Use either method of designing, but use tempera paint or watercolor as the color medium.
3. Use just black or one color on white to form the design and do not color in the spaces. This will create a line design.

Lesson Eight: Stop! Look! Listen!

MELTED CRAYON AND PAINT

STOP! DON'T THROW AWAY THOSE BROKEN CRAYons! Look! They can be shaved into tiny pieces! Listen! Exclamations of fun and surprise!

That box of old crayons you've been saving and wondering what to do with will come in handy. Let's make some gay flower sprays, or autumn trees, or tropical birds, or whatever else that comes to mind.

Decide what it is that *you* want to create. Then choose crayons of several different colors that are appropriate to whatever you are going to make. Now let's begin. Open a pair of scissors so that the blades are as far apart as possible. Then use the scissors as a scraping tool, peeling off a layer of crayon. Let the shavings fall on a large piece of newsprint. Continue until you think you have enough color on the paper to make an interesting picture.

95

Perhaps you were able to drop the crayon shavings so that they landed in the approximate shape of the flower, or tree, or bird, or whatever. If so, fine—just leave them where they are. Possibly you need to move them just a bit in order to resemble somewhat the shape of whatever you have in mind. If mine is going to be a flower, I'll move some so that most of the colored shavings are where the blossom is going to be. There—that makes me think of a group of flowers. A little green, perhaps two shades of green, somewhat lower down will become a leaf later on. Don't worry about it not being the exact shape—just get it in about the right place.

Of course, the crayon is just laying on the paper, and if we moved the paper the crayon would all fall off. So let's fix that! Carefully lay a piece of newspaper over the crayon shavings. Then with a warm iron press the whole thing. Not too long—just enough to melt the wax crayon. Remove the newspaper, and look at that! The crayon not only sticks to the paper now, but the colors have spread and blended together. Pretty, isn't it, but it's only half done—so let's finish it!

Look at the arrangement of color again. See, there's the group of flowers and the leaf. Oh, sure, the edges are uneven and some extra color scattered in other places—but that's what makes it interesting. With a watercolor brush and black paint—either tempera or water-color—quickly sketch in the outline of the petals, the leaf, a stem. See, there it is, color that moves around, yet with the idea held together by the lines sketched over it.

You'll find the finished pictures are more exciting than if they were meticulously drawn and colored in with new crayons. Display the finished picture and they will prove that those old crayons still have lots of life in them.

Make It Easy—for Yourself!

1. Have the children remove all the paper before scraping the crayons.
2. Prepare a place for ironing near an electric outlet. Have a thick layer of newspaper that the heat won't go through. Use it as an ironing board.
3. Near the ironing area, have newspapers to be used for pressing over the crayon.
4. Use pieces of heavy cardboard as trays for carrying ma-terials to the ironing area. One piece for every six or

eight children is enough, as they will have to take turns to iron.

5. Set up one area of the room with desks or tables for painting. Cover the work area with newspaper. Provide several brushes, paint (watercolor or tempera), and a container of water. After the crayon shavings have been pressed, let children take turns at sketching in their pictures.

Variations

1. Use black paint to add additional parts to the picture: for example, to a picture of an autumn tree not only the trunk and branches of the one tree might be sketched, but smaller trees in the background, and a house in the distance.
2. Make a landscape picture. Use crayon shavings to indicate the color of the several things in the picture. Then use paint to sketch each part of the landscape.
3. Make a still life arrangement. Use this crayon and paint method to interpret it.
4. Let the crayon shavings drop anywhere on the paper without previous thought of what is to be made. Then look at the results carefully. See if an idea can be "found" in the pressed crayon. Sketch it in with paint.

Variation for Lower Grades

Use crayon shavings and iron as previously described. Sketch in the various parts of the picture with crayon.

CHALK (5)

CHARCOAL

CHAPTER **5**   *Chalk and Charcoal*

Lesson One: Don't Eliminate the Negative

CHALK STENCILS

ACCENTUATE THE POSITIVE, BUT DON'T ELIMINATE the negative! This could be our slogan for this lesson, for the negative is just as good as the positive when you're talking about—or singing about, if you like—chalk stencils. This time we'll use the chalk as a powder rather than in stick form like a crayon.

Why use a stencil? Because it's a wonderful way to create interesting repetition in a picture. The same original pattern—or stencil—can be used over and over again, and the result is always the distinctive clean-cut edge characteristic of a stencil. But even in repetition there can be variety—if you *don't* eliminate the negative.

So let's start by making a stencil—a very simple one, because in this lesson we're going to experiment to see how many ways we can use the two parts of a stencil—the positive and the negative. Draw any geometric or simple free-form shape. Cut out the shape, leaving the paper around it intact. This outside piece of paper, with the hole in it where the shape was cut out, is the negative form of the stencil. Save it. Don't eliminate the negative! Use this part of the stencil to draw the same shape over again, this time cutting off the outside part so as to leave the shape—the *positive* form of the stencil—in one piece. This two-step process is necessary when cutting with a pair of scissors rather than with a stencil knife. But it is easy to do, and it takes very little time to get both forms of the stencil—the shape itself and the hole where the shape was originally.

Now we're ready to experiment. The first two ways of using a stencil are easy enough, aren't they? All you have to do is apply chalk to each part—the positive and the negative—separately. Wrap facial tissue around your index finger and push the chalk powder from the stencil onto the paper. The supply of chalk may be made on a "palette" paper by rubbing a small area of the paper with chalk, or drawing a chalk line near the edge of the stencil and having your chalk powder supply right on the stencil itself. Either way works fine. Just apply the chalk dust sparingly so as to color the paper only, without leaving extra residue to become smudged.

So far the experiment has resulted in only two different forms. But now let's overlap the positive and the negative. Rub the chalk from both parts of the stencil. See, a new way of using the stencil—it looks as if one is in back of the other. But is that the only way of using the two parts of the stencil together? Not at all! Make the two parts look transparent (by rubbing the chalk off one stencil, then removing it from the paper and placing the other stencil partly over the first rubbing. Repeat the rubbing process.) Can you think of any other ways of using the two parts of the stencil so as to create a new effect? (Try reversing the placement of the stencils.)

Use only one color chalk for all this experimentation, and arrange each of the parts so as to make an interesting all-over design. Then complete the picture by adding a second or third color, repeating each of the stencil experiments or choosing which ones to repeat in order to make the most interesting effect.

Chalk used this way results in designs of special delicacy. You'll display them proudly—and want to try powdered chalk and stencils again.

Make It Easy—for Yourself!

1. Use pieces of scrap paper—anything as firm as construction paper—about 6 x 9 as palettes. Have children rub their colored chalk over a small area. This will give a supply of powdered chalk. (Another simple way of applying the chalk is to draw a chalk line close to the edge of the stencil. Use it to wipe off onto the paper.)

2. Give each child a piece of facial tissue. Use it wrapped around the index finger as an applicator for the powdered chalk.

3. Always apply the chalk away from the stencil. This gives a clean, sharp edge and prevents the chalk from going underneath the stencil.

4. Apply very little powdered chalk to the design. It should only color the paper. Any surplus chalk is unnecessary and becomes a nuisance.

5. Be sure to leave plenty of area around the negative form of the stencil—at least an inch—to prevent the chalk from going off the edge of the stencil.

6. A small piece of clean scrap paper to rest the fingers on while holding the picture will keep dirty fingers from making smudges on the picture.

Variations

1. Use several kinds of geometric or free-form shapes. Overlap them, using the negatives and positives of the stencils. Arrange colors to complete a well-designed non-objective picture.

2. Let each child write his name large. Cut it out leaving a little space on each side of the writing to create a name stencil. Each time turn the stencil in a different direction before the chalk is applied. Create an all-over pattern in this way.

3. Make a stencil of a real object. Use it again and again to complete an all-over design picture.

4. Cut out shapes of several real things and arrange them as a picture. Use the same stencils several times in the same picture in order to create an interesting rhythm through repetition.

5. Vary the size of the paper to create a tall, thin picture or a long, narrow picture. Also, try chalk on colored construction paper as well as on white paper.

Variations for Lower Grades

1. Lay the stencil under a piece of newsprint. Rub over it with the flat side of a piece of chalk. Move the stencil about under the paper until the picture is completed. Use powdered chalk of another color applied with a piece of facial tissue to all the plain areas of the paper.
2. Cut a piece of oaktag or other heavy paper into many shapes. Vary the sizes, and make some plain shapes and some fancy shapes. Arrange them in a pleasing way, overlapping some. Lay a piece of newsprint over the arrangement. Apply one or more colors by rubbing over it with the flat side of chalk. Finish all plain areas by adding powdered chalk with a piece of facial tissue.

OBJECTIVES

1. To offer an easy form of accidental art expression.

2. To introduce a new technique in mixed media.

3. To offer a fool-proof art lesson for every child in the classroom.

(For grades 4 through 6)

Lesson Two: Let's Be Tacky!

WET PAPER AND CHALK

HAVE YOU EVER HEARD IT SAID THAT MANY MAS-terpieces were accidents? That is, the artist began by attempting something, but the results were not what he had attempted, yet were more beautiful and more to his liking. Another form of art work is one of pure accident; that is, the exact results can not be predicted. This form of expression is sometimes frowned on as not being "thought out" or creative. However, the results can be satisfying, the process easy, and the young artist is not frustrated, for there is no chance of mistakes. It also makes for interesting variety in an art program, and is a good way of introducing new media and techniques. One such form of accidental art is done with chalk and starch. It's a tacky technique, so, let's be tacky!

The most important aspect of this lesson is color, and care should be taken to encourage students to choose three colors which they like together. In this way the lesson contains thought and creativity, and it is not entirely accidental. When we have chosen our three pieces of colored chalk, it is time to arrange our colors in any pattern until they completely cover a piece of 12 x 18 white paper which has been

104

folded lengthwise and then reopened. The color may be applied in large blocks, wide bands, diamond shapes, circles, any way at all as long as the paper is covered with brilliant tones of chalk. Using the side of the chalk covers a wide area smoothly and thickly.

Now that our color has been applied, it's time to get tacky. Using thick liquid starch, we brush it on over the entire surface design, keeping it fairly thick. We let it stand for a minute while we clean our brushes, allowing the starch to become slightly tacky. Now we refold our paper, and with our fingers (or with any object) we press down, making more design patterns. This pressure makes the starch move about, creating the design. When we open our paper, we find our chalk design glowing beneath a textured cover. When the starch dries it creates an illusion of tinted glass over color.

This simple lesson is fun and produces marvelous examples of accidental art.

Make It Easy—for Yourself!

1. Cover the desks with newspaper.
2. Have the class practice applying chalk on smaller pieces of paper. This is to help determine whether the choice of color is pleasing and to help create an interesting pattern.
3. Arrange the class into small groups and distribute a small container of starch to each group.
4. Use wide brushes (if available) to apply the starch. Wash them as soon as possible after use. One brush for a group is enough.

Variations

1. Create a non-objective picture. Apply liquid starch (may be diluted with up to an equal amount of water) to a 12 x 18 manila or white drawing paper. Apply chalk while the starch is still wet. Apply in free, rhythmic motions. Overlap lines, fill in areas, blend colors with the top of your finger. The starch will make it easy to blend the colors and will act as a fixative when the picture is dry.
2. Create a still life or other realistic picture. Apply liquid starch (diluted with water if desired). Then apply chalk, mixing and blending the colors as desired.

Lesson Three: Swing Out That Rhythm!

CHALK TO MUSIC

LET'S LISTEN TO SOME MUSIC. HEAR THE LONG gliding sounds, the sharp high notes, the low booms. Notice that change in speed—the slow quiet tones, then the faster rhythm. Listen again. This time use your hand to swing out that rhythm! Pretend you have a piece of chalk. Move your hand with the music, just as though lines and color were being left on a paper.

But why pretend! Pass out large pieces of manila or white drawing paper. Let each child choose several colors of chalk—colors which to him represent the moods of the music. As the musical selection is replayed, swing out that chalk to the rhythm of the music. Let it move rapidly or slowly as the pace changes; let it rise or fall the way the tones do; let the color change as the mood of the music

106

changes. Let color and line reproduce tone and rhythm. Leave only lines for some parts of the music but fill other areas with chalk.

After the music has stopped add details which will unify and complete the picture. Repeat some of the lines and shapes in the design. Turn the paper in different directions so that the repeated parts will be in various sections of the paper.

There it is—music in visual form, so that we can look at it instead of listening to it. There is the same rhythm, tone, accent, mood. Look at it again. Can you "hear" the music coming from your chalk pictures? Certainly you can! Display them along with the name of the music so that others will also "see" the music.

Make It Easy—for Yourself!

1. Choose a musical selection which has frequent changes in rhythm and tonal quality.
2. Play the entire piece or selected portions several times before attempting any visual interpretation. Talk about the sound. Get the children to express their thoughts in *visual* words rather than *sound* words. For example: light instead of quiet; short instead of quick. This will help them to make the transition from sound to sight.
3. Encourage children to use their hands either in the air or on their desks to interpret the line and the rhythm of the music. This will make them more free with their motions when they use chalk.
4. Cover all work areas with newspaper to protect desks from the chalk.
5. Limit the number of colors used to three or four. This will permit variety without creating undue problems because of too frequent changes of chalk.

Variations

1. Make a more realistic interpretation of the music. Tell the story of the music, or let the children express their own ideas of what the music says.
2. Use other media to interpret the music. With the younger children it might be crayon, and with the older children it might be watercolor.

Lesson Four: One and One Are— a Landscape!

LANDSCAPES

ONE AND ONE ARE—A LANDSCAPE! AT LEAST that's the right answer if it's one piece of charcoal and one piece of colored chalk—with a dash of careful looking—all thoughtfully mixed on a piece of white drawing paper. There you have the ingredients for a new art lesson that will be fun to do and good to look at.

Let's start with the looking. What do you see from your classroom windows? Rolling hills as the background for a rural scene? Or tenement houses crushed by outmoded factories? Or suburban ranch-style homes dotting the landscape among newly-planted trees and manicured hedges? Whatever it is, take a closer look. Find one limited area that you could develop into a picture of a peaceful countryside, a crowded city street, a growing residential area. Don't try to include too much—keep the area small so that you can make each important part big in your picture.

Look for the most important lines. Sketch them on quickly with a piece of charcoal. Keep them big; make them divide the paper into large and small areas. Put in only those things which tell the story of what you see. Choose carefully to make a well-balanced, organized whole that lets your eye move easily from one part of your picture to another. Leave out—for the present—all distracting details.

Now you have the main part of that landscape down on a piece of paper. But it's all in black and white. Let's perk it up with a little color—any color—and one is enough, for this first time at least. Take the blue chalk, for example. Lightly add a little to the rolling hills in the distance, or whatever is a large area in your picture. But use it sparingly. It isn't a crayon—don't just fill in the whole area with blue. Let the chalk merely suggest that there is a solid area, that it is basically a horizontal line. Rub it slightly with the tip of your finger. See, it softens the color, smooths and blends the harsh edges.

Next add a little of the same color to a vertical mass. Again, merely let it suggest the direction of a solid area. Leave lots of white paper in that vertical section. Soften the color by blending it into the paper.

Looks more interesting already, doesn't it? What else should have a suggestion of color? Place the color so that it helps your eye to move easily from one part of the picture to another. Hold your picture as far away from you as possible. Look carefully. Where else is a little color needed? Well, let's put it there, then! But, take it easy—don't overdo it!

Last of all, sketch in those interesting details you left out until now. So back to the charcoal again. The tiny branches against an empty sky, the smoke curling up from a chimney, the broken window on the second floor of the store, the ———, whatever the details are that will complete your picture.

There you are—one piece of charcoal and one piece of chalk equals a landscape all ready to be displayed.

Make It Easy—for Yourself!

1. If working outdoors, tape a 12 x 18 paper to a drawing board. A large piece of heavy cardboard will serve as a fine substitute. If working indoors, cover the desks with newspaper to protect them from the chalk and charcoal.

2. Limit the number of colors of chalk to be used. One color is enough. The color is merely to add interest to the charcoal drawing—don't overdo it.
3. Each person should have an eraser. A kneaded eraser is best for cleaning up chalk or charcoal, but a gum eraser or even a pencil eraser will do a satisfactory job.
4. No pencils—do all sketching in charcoal.
5. Emphasize the importance of open areas in a chalk and charcoal drawing. This is a drawing, and lines are important. Do not try to imitate a painting.
6. Spray finished pictures with a fixative to give a light coating if they are to be displayed where there is the possibility of something rubbing against them.

Variations

1. Make chalk and charcoal pictures using other subject matter: still life, portraits, abstracts.
2. Use two or three colors of chalk to block in areas of color in a landscape. Don't draw anything—no mountains, houses, trees. Instead, use chalk to make flat masses of color approximately the size and shape of the mountains, houses, trees. When this is finished, use charcoal to sketch in these same parts of the picture. Sketch over the colored areas without trying to match them exactly. The emphasis is on color, with sketching merely to catch or hold an impression.

OBJECTIVES

1. **To provide opportunity for an exercise in basic drawing.**

2. **To encourage closer observation of common objects.**

3. **To provide opportunity for using a combination of art media that are not ordinarily used together.**

4. **To introduce charcoal as a new medium.**

5. **To use watercolor as a flat wash.**

6. **To use shading to create a three-dimensional effect on a two-dimensional plane.**

(For grades 5 and 6)

Lesson Five: "A-B-C-D, E-F-G . . ."

STILL LIFE WITH CHARCOAL AND WATERCOLOR

STILL LIFE IS TO ART AS THE ALPHABET IS TO SPELLing. It is fundamental, necessary, and can be used in a multitude of ways, creating exciting results through meaningful learning experiences.

Variations using still life range from basic drawing exercises to inspiration for abstract interpretation. One of the most effective steps along the way makes use of charcoal and watercolor.

Approach this lesson as a drawing exercise, emphasizing to the class that drawing an object is really very simple if enough care is taken to study what is being drawn. Look for the uniqueness of the object and its variations of outline. For example, every apple is different, and an analysis of two or more will show in what ways they differ. They are not perfectly round or symmetrical, and if the artist can see the differences in outline he can capture them on paper.

Choose your still life materials very carefully. Find simple and unadorned objects which are close to geometric shapes. More complex pieces may be added when the class has had more drawing experience. For the first part of this lesson do not group your still life materials, but rather spread them out across the room so that each student may choose one object to draw on a 9 x 12 piece of white drawing paper.

Before doing any drawing let's discover some of the properties that are characteristic of charcoal. The most obvious quality is that of smudging, and this can be used very effectively in creating a three-dimensional look to the drawn object. In order to make a round object appear to have depth, it is necessary to give it a highlight (the part closest to the light source). A gradual darkening from this white spot to the outside edges will make those edges seem to retreat. This contrast from white to a gradual darkening to black at the edges will give the object its three-dimensional look. Smudging the charcoal with the fingers can help to achieve this important transition from light to dark.

After each student has chosen the article he wishes to draw, have him carefully proceed by first studying the object and then trying to very lightly reproduce its outline with charcoal on the 9 x 12 paper. When the student feels he has captured the "look" of the article, he then proceeds to give it life by shading it dark to light. After a good black and white drawing has been produced, the next step is to give it a pale tint of color with watercolors.

Drop a small amount of color into a puddle of clear water to produce a pastel wash. Load the brush with this color, tip the white paper toward you, and paint a band of color at the top of the shape. Overlap the next band so that the excess water will be carried down and continue, band by band, until the object is colored. The charcoal which is now fixed by the paint shows through the color and creates the desired shadowing.

This one object on the 9 x 12 paper is for practice. Now put your still life materials into a group and repeat the lesson on a larger sheet of paper. According to time limitations, this project may become as many as four independent lessons by dividing it into drawing and painting activities. It is an ideal lesson in that it is both informative and ideal for display purposes.

Make It Easy—for Yourself!

1. Give out watercolor materials at the beginning of the lesson so that each student may work at his own rate of speed during the practice session.
2. Break charcoal sticks in half for easier handling.
3. Place objects for practice drawing in various parts of the room for easy viewing.
4. Place still life arrangement at a high level.
5. No pencils—do all drawing with the charcoal.

Variations

1. Use charcoal only for a drawing lesson.
2. Use this as a drawing lesson in any medium—pencil, chalk, crayon.
3. Cut out shapes without any previous drawing. Then color and group them together.
4. Make an abstract of the still life arrangement, use the combination of charcoal and watercolor.
5. Use the charcoal and watercolor technique for a landscape drawing.

6.
CUT
PAPER

CHAPTER **6**   *Cut Paper*

Lesson One: A Classroom Drama

REALISTIC PICTURES

TEACHER: WHY IS THAT COW STANDING ON THE fence, Johnny?

JOHNNY: (indignantly) He's not! He's behind it!

TEACHER: Well, why didn't you put the fence in front of him?

JOHNNY: I did! That's why I put the cow high on my paper.

TEACHER: But, Johnny, he's bigger than your fence. We know that things far away look smaller.

JOHNNY: He's not far away. He's just behind the fence!

TEACHER: All right, Johnny. That's very nice.

(Curtain)

A typical scene? Perhaps. Johnny is beginning to think about how things should look in his picture, but as yet he doesn't understand things like distance or that objects sometimes block out parts of other objects when they are in the foreground. It would be too confusing

116

and frustrating to Johnny if adult concepts were forced on him too soon, and yet we would like to have him discover object relationships for himself. What to do? Well, let's try teaching Johnny a new word and applying it to a picture. The word? *Overlapping*. The picture? A cut paper composition.

Cut out about five simple shapes for a demonstration. These can be fish, birds, bottles, vases, anything at all. Explain to the class what overlapping means—something in front of or on top of something else.

Holding up two pieces of different-colored paper side by side, ask if they overlap. The answer, of course, is no. Next move the papers so that one is in front of the other, and again ask if they overlap. When the class understands what the term means, ask which piece of paper is closest to them. We can tell because the piece of paper which covers the other piece is entirely visible while the one in back is blocked out, and so must be farther back.

Next take your five cut-outs and paste two side by side on a piece of 12 x 18 drawing paper. We can't tell if either one is closer until we overlap a third object on the other two. We can easily see that now number three is closer because it blocks out part of the other two. Continue to paste the objects down, one by one, overlapping something each time, and have the class decide which is closer to them.

Now that we know the principle, let's put it into practice. On a 12 x 18 piece of white paper, have the class make a cut paper picture in which at least two things overlap. The subject doesn't matter—it can be left up to each child. You will be amazed at how much the class will enjoy this new adventure, but this enjoyment also leads to difficulties. Watch the class carefully because in their excitement they tend to overlap too much and spoil their original idea. They must be cautioned not to overlap a large piece entirely over a smaller one and completely hide it.

This simple lesson results in a great deal of learning. The concepts of space, object relationships, and distance will carry over into other media as Johnny begins to "see" as well as feel his picture development. You will be delighted at the new sophistication and beauty of the work.

Make It Easy—for Yourself!

1. Cover desks with newspaper.
2. Work on large 12 x 18 paper.

3. Have separated colors of 9 x 12 paper in several parts of the room.
4. Have each row go to the nearest 9 x 12 colored paper and choose two colors to begin their pictures.
5. Let the class share colors while they use them.
6. Each child should have his own scissors and paste.
7. Distribute the paste on small pieces of paper which can be disposed of later.

Variation

After the initial experience of this lesson with cut paper, vary it by using other media (crayon, paint, or a combination of them).

Variations for K

1. Discuss overlapping and then have the class create torn paper designs using free form shapes in which each piece must overlap another. This produces a unified design. Limit the colors to two on a dark or white background.
2. Use this same idea with mixed papers (foil, tissue, wrapping paper) for a more dramatic look.

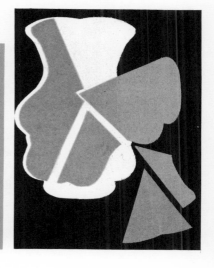

OBJECTIVES

1. **To give a basic understanding of abstract art.**

2. **To increase appreciation of abstract art.**

3. **To give a sense of achievement by being able to create abstract art.**

4. **To show abstract design is not always accidental.**

   (For grades 5 and 6)

Lesson Two: Paper Picasso!

ABSTRACTING A FORM

ACCIDENTAL DESIGNS ARE FINE WHEN EXPERIMENT-ing with a new medium, but good designs are thought out and planned. Even non-objective painting is thought out in terms of color, contrast, mood, balance, harmony, variety, and repetition. Have you ever tried taking a realistic shape or form and turning it into an abstract design? Sound complicated and difficult? It isn't. It's very simple and very informative. Try it. It can be approached in many ways.

Give your class a good old-fashioned drawing lesson! Place some objects that have simple shapes in different parts of the room and have the class draw them. Talk about drawing as a means of putting on paper something that your eye sees. Discuss curves, angles, straight lines, and point them out on the objects on display. Let the class draw them, each child choosing the one he likes best. Urge them to draw large. Don't use pencils, for this often leads to small, tight drawings. Crayons are good if they are used lightly. Tell the class that these drawings will be cut out, so mistakes can be ignored or eliminated.

When the drawing is finished, it is then cut out and traced on two different colors of construction paper. You now have three identical shapes, one that you drew with crayon, the other two on colored construction paper. Here is the problem which the class must solve: to create an abstract design from the two paper cut outs. This can be accomplished in several ways. One shape can be left whole while the other is cut into a few free-form shapes. You can place all of these (the whole and cut up objects) on a piece of paper, and arrange them until you have made a pleasing abstract design. Some pieces may be overlapped while others are separated. It's your choice. It may be better to start by placing a larger shape on the paper and arranging the smaller pieces to compliment it. The abstract may also be mounted with the original realistic drawing to show its source of inspiration.

Another approach is to have the original object made by folding a piece of 9 x 12 paper in half and cutting out half a shape around the fold. When the paper is unfolded you have a whole shape perfectly symmetrical from which you may begin your abstract design.

You, too, can be a Picasso with paper!

Make It Easy—for Yourself!

1. Use objects with simple shapes, such as bottles and vases.
2. Cover all work areas with newspaper.
3. Have a wide choice of colored paper from which to choose.
4. Work large—plan the abstraction on 12 x 18 paper.
5. The teacher may collect scraps of paper as she walks around the room. This provides more work area and also makes for a quicker and more orderly clean-up.
6. Collect the scissors as children finish using them—for more work space and simpler clean-up.
7. Distribute paste on a scrap of paper that can be disposed of later.

Variations

1. Cut out many different realistic objects (houses, people, animals). Arrange by overlapping them in varying directions creating an abstract design.
2. Cut out several objects all related to one theme (such as music, games, or hobbies). Arrange them to create an abstract picture.
3. Cut out many of the same object (same size or varying sizes) and arrange them by overlapping in varying directions to cover the whole paper. Use paper cutter to trim finished picture for even edges.

OBJECTIVES

1. To use construction paper in a big and bold way.

2. To create a design within a design.

3. To help foster the idea that a picture may be both real and unreal at the same time.

(For grades 4 through 6, adapted to grades 1 through 3)

Lesson Three: A Carnival in Your Room!

ANIMAL MOSAGE

WOULD YOU LIKE TO HAVE BIG ANIMALS DONE IN gay splashes of color—a carnival in your room?

Begin by thinking of things that are alive and can move from place to place. They might be cats, dogs, rabbits, fish, butterflies—or anything else that is real and can move about. Use chalk to draw your real living thing. Make it as large as possible on 18 x 24 construction paper. Use a dull or dark colored paper—grey, black, brown. Then cut it out.

So far the animals or other living things look very real, but the next step is to make them "unreal." Do this by making each one into a *mosage*—a combination of mosaic and collage. Choose several varieties of colored construction paper—half sheets of 9 x 12 paper will be enough. Cut them into simple shapes of various sizes. Then arrange

122

them, overlapping them inside the real, living thing. All at once they become entirely unreal but more intriguing. When a pleasing arrangement has been made, paste all the parts onto the whole.

Your classroom will take on a carnival air as each creature is displayed—each very much alive but very unreal.

Make It Easy—for Yourself!

1. Get a good variety of real, living things by having the class suggest many possibilities before they begin work.
2. Use chalk for the drawing because it encourages bigness. Keep all the chalk drawing on one side of the paper only. Then as many changes as are needed can be made. Turn the picture over to the clean side to paste on the colored shapes.
3. If the colored construction paper is cut in straight lines only, it will be easier for the class to handle and will result in better designs.
4. Have the 9 x 12 colored construction paper cut in half (6 x 9). Give each child three or four colors and allow them to choose one or two others. This will permit variety and individual choice without too much difficulty of distribution of materials.
5. Collect the scrap paper after the big, real creature has been cut out. This will permit more work area free of unnecessary materials.

Variations

1. Cut a smaller size shape, either real or non-objective, from 12 x 18 construction paper. Cut contrasting colors of construction paper into small pieces and arrange as a mosaic. Do not overlap the parts but leave a narrow space between each piece in typical mosaic form.
2. Create a collage (a design made from applied pieces of various materials) using one or more colors of construction paper along with newspaper, corrugated paper, cardboard, or other available kinds of paper for accent or contrast.

Variation for Lower Grades

From a piece of 12 x 18 construction paper cut a picture of a favorite or imaginary animal. Add contrasting colored construction paper for more interest. This could be to make it either more real or more imaginary.

Lesson Four: Tall, of Course!

EXAGGERATED PICTURES

ARE YOU TIRED OF TINY PICTURES CROWDED DOWN at the bottom of the paper. Do you want a simple remedy? Just cut the paper in half the tall way—and have a day when you make them tall!

Have an assortment of 18 x 24 colored and white construction paper that has been cut in half. Just the sight of a tall paper only nine inches wide but 24 inches tall is exciting. Talk about what could be a tall picture. Oh, a skyscraper, of course—but couldn't other things be tall, too? What would a man look like to a bug in the grass? Tall! Of course! What would a sailboat look like to a sardine? Tall! Of course! What would a cat look like to an ant? Tall! Of course!

So think of what you want to make, whether it's a cat or a tree or a clown. Then pretend it's made of rubber and think of what it would look like if you stretched it taller and taller until it came all the way to the top of the paper. Choose several papers of contrasting colors. Cut out a tall, skinny rabbit, or flower, or rooster. Make one or two somewhat shorter ones. Then arrange them on the tall, narrow paper, overlapping the several stretched out objects so that they make a pleasing picture.

Be sure to give the picture a title. That's part of the fun. Remember—there's magic in a half sheet of paper, so make them tall!

Make It Easy—for Yourself!

1. Have a large assortment of colored construction paper cut to 9 x 24.
2. Constantly stress making things tall—stretch them out TALL. Exaggerate.
3. No pencil drawing first. That tends to make things small instead of tall. Just "think" your picture—then cut.
4. As you walk about the room, collect the scrap paper and the scissors after the tall objects have been cut. This provides more work space and makes for a quicker and more orderly clean-up.

Variation

Use a combination of materials to make a tall picture: construction paper (9 x 24) and cloth; construction paper and paint.

Variation for Lower Grades

Paint a tall picture. Use the familiar tempera paint—stretch the picture from the top to the bottom of the 9 x 24 paper.

OBJECTIVES

1. To introduce weaving concepts to young children.

2. To use color and line to create original and unique designs by weaving.

3. To teach color contrast, rhythm, and unity through weaving.

(For grades 2 through 4, adapted to grades 5 and 6)

Lesson Five: Rhythmic Chant

PAPER WEAVING

IN, OUT, IN, OUT, UP, UNDER, UP, UNDER—IS often the rhythmic chant found in an absorbing and challenging lesson on paper weaving. Now wait! Don't turn up your nose or turn the page. This simple lesson can be fun and exciting by adding a little imagination. It can also be correlated with social studies and other subjects. Try it!

This seemingly easy concept of warp and woof or in and out can be confusing and difficult for the young child, and so should be presented slowly and in stages of development. Let's begin with the most simple example of paper weaving—plain weaving in two colors which will result in the traditional checker board pattern.

Using two sheets of 9 x 12 construction paper of different colors, cut one sheet into one inch strips nine inches long. On the other

127

sheet mark a one inch border on one end of the paper. Fold this sheet in half and mark off one inch lines from one edge to the other. The lines will run from the fold to the drawn border. Beginning at the fold, cut these lines down to the border. Open up the sheet of paper and you have a paper loom with one inch warp threads. Now all you have to do is weave in your one inch woof strips, remembering that if you began by going over the first strip, your next piece must go under the first strip. With this traditional pattern you can also introduce color contrast, monochromatic color schemes (two shades of one color), and warm and cool colors.

Don't be surprised if your class has trouble understanding how to weave for at first this simple procedure can be quite confusing. This is why it is wise to start with this simple, straight weaving and to chant up, under, up, under as you go along.

Now let's add a little spice to our designs! Using the same basic principle as in the straight weaving, we can achieve some marvelous effects by just using a little variation. Let's try a larger sheet of paper for our loom, 12 x 18, and two sheets of 9 x 12 construction paper for our woof. These three colors should be chosen carefully, remembering that a variety of light, dark, and bright makes for interesting contrast. We can be in a patriotic mood with red, white, and blue; or in a holiday mood with red, green, and white; or in a cool mood with blue, green, and violet; or in a warm mood with red, orange, and yellow; or in a creative mood with any colors we like together. We can also achieve a feeling with what we do with our loom, for the pattern can be rhythmic, geometric, or abstract. Let's see how.

Once again we mark a one inch border along one end of the 12 x 18 paper, then fold it in half with the border up. Instead of marking off the strips, we now cut free-hand from the fold down to the border. Don't cut straight. Try cutting flowing curved lines, or jagged zig zag lines, or a combination of both. These cuts will create a pattern in the finished design. Vary the width of the twelve inch strips cut from the 9 x 12 papers. This will also vary the pattern as the wide and narrow strips are interwoven with the curved or jagged cut lines. The results are truly startling and the variety of patterns is exciting.

The progress of this type of weaving may be slower than straight weaving, for the abstract lines of the design require greater concentration. Don't be discouraged, for all at once the light will shine and the bells will ring as your chant of in, out, up, and under will find its mark in young minds.

Make It Easy—for Yourself!

1. When doing straight weaving with very young children, pre-cut the strips on a paper cutter.
2. Arrange paper in piles by color. Let each child decide which colors he will use before he goes up to get them.
3. Prepare your own sample to show the class to illustrate better the goal which is to be reached.
4. Make sure that each strip is tight against the one preceding it so that the finished design will hold together well.
5. The edges of the woven strips may be pasted to keep them fastened more securely.

Variations

1. Use different materials woven in with the paper (raffia, yarn, strips of fabric, novelty papers such as gift wrappings.
2. Use the woven design as a background for a cut-out shape or picture which can be pasted onto it.

Variations for Upper Grades

1. Use paper weaving as a lead into fabric weaving with yarn, roving, cloth.
2. Use paper weaving in limited areas to produce unusual effects—for example: borders on placemats.

Lesson Six: Have You Ever Seen a Horbit?

IMAGINARY ANIMALS

HAVE YOU EVER HEARD OF A STRANGE ANIMAL called a liog—or a deehant?

Ask your class that some day. Write the two names on the blackboard. Perhaps one child will wonder if liog could be part lion and part dog. Then it quickly follows that deehant is part deer and part elephant. Have the class think of two other animals that are very different. Write the names of them on the blackboard next to each other: for example, HORSE—RABBIT. Make a new name from them—one that is interesting sounding. Perhaps it will be *horbit*.

Let the class talk about what a *horbit* would look like. What part of him would look like a horse? What part of him would look like a rabbit? Now they are ready to "create" a new animal of their own, one which they keep a secret from everyone but you, their teacher.

On a scrap of paper have them write the names of two very different animals, then combine them for a new animal—just as you did on the blackboard. Take a peek at each scrap of paper to see that they have the right idea. Then while enthusiasm is high, let them go to work.

Have an assortment of colored construction paper from which various parts of the new animal may be cut. Let them choose one or many colors. Remember that this is not a real animal, so of course there is no reason for trying to make the colors realistic. Choose any colors that look well together. Attach all the parts to make the new animal, add any deails for finishing touches, and then see if the other children can tell what he is.

Make It Easy—for Yourself!

1. Have an assortment of colored construction paper in several places about the classroom so that there will never be many children choosing paper from any one place at a time.
2. If possible, use staplers to attach the various parts of the new animal. That will eliminate the need for passing out paste, and will make it possible to concentrate more completely on the creation of an original idea.
3. Don't use pencils for any pre-drawing—they would hinder freedom of expression.

Variation

Use other materials with the construction paper: cloth, pipe cleaners, wire, yarn.

Variation for Lower Grades

Tell a simple story about an animal that changed himself partly into something else. Have the children draw with crayons or paint a picture of what he looked like.

Variations for Higher Grades

1. Make the new animal three-dimensional.
2. Try to capture in the new animal the qualities you think of with each (speed, gentleness, laziness) as well as their physical appearance.

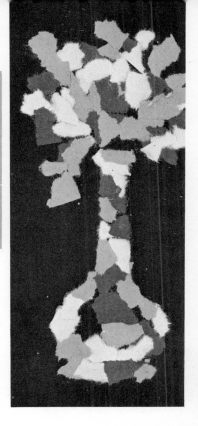

Lesson Seven: Inside Out

BUILDING A PICTURE WITH TORN PAPER

WHEN YOU MAKE A PICTURE, HOW DO YOU START? Do you start by drawing a line which travels around, meets itself, and makes a picture of something? This is outlining and is a common way to draw. It is not, however, the only way. Some artists work from the inside out, building up volume to create form. To introduce this concept to children, we use a familiar medium, construction paper.

Use a variety of colors, tearing them into small pieces, similar to large pieces of confetti. Near the center of a 12 x 18 sheet of dark paper paste a piece of "confetti." This is the inside. Now, by overlapping every additional piece, our picture grows and grows. Make

133

sure you add pieces all around the first one so that we will not create a line.

As our shape grows and grows and gets fatter and fatter we can try to see what it could be. What does it remind you of? That one looks like a person's face. This one looks like a colorful fish. That square one looks like a building. When we have decided what we are going to make, we can add pieces in the right directions so that our form will take its finished shape.

When the picture is finished, add details (eyes, mouth, belt) by cutting them out of black or dark paper in order to contrast them with the colors of our shapes.

This lesson stimulates creative thinking as the young artist concentrates on making a picture from the inside out.

Make It Easy—for Yourself!

1. Have 9 x 12 paper pre-cut to 4½ x 6.
2. Let each child choose three or more colors.
3. Cover desks with newspapers.
4. Begin by tearing only a few pieces of each color. More can be torn as they are needed. This makes it easier to keep the room orderly and makes for better working conditions.
5. Distribute paste on small pieces of scrap paper. The torn pieces may be dabbed on the paste.

Variations

1. Finish picture with solid cut paper shapes.
2. Finish picture with an unrelated medium: crayon, paint, chalk.

Variation for Lower Grades

Start with a puddle of paint and build an object by pushing the paint from the inside out.

Variation for Grades 5–6

Draw each object from the inside out, using a scribbling motion. Use chalk, crayon, charcoal, or any other lineal medium.

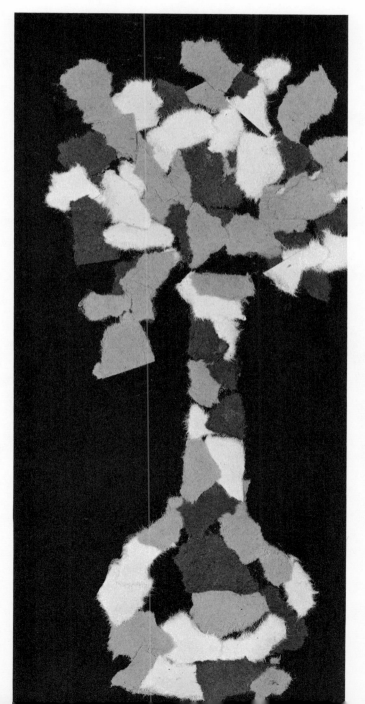

CHAPTER **7**

Fabric

Lesson One: Cloth on Cloth

CLOTH PICTURES

YOU'VE MADE PICTURES WITH PAINT AND WITH crayon and with paper. But have you ever thought of making them with cloth—*on* cloth? Instead of a new idea, let's stick to an old idea with a new twist—or more exactly, an old idea with new materials.

Get together a box of assorted materials—scraps of cloth, felt, yarn, cotton roving, even colored pipe cleaners. Cut burlap into pieces about 9 x 12 or a little larger. Scissors and a jar of paste complete all the materials necessary to make cloth pictures—all the materials, that is, except a liberal amount of imagination which is always on call.

Talk about making the picture as though it was to be done with any other material: make something big and important first; fill the paper (burlap in this case); have the picture tell something. Then let scissors, paste, imagination, and materials go to work.

Typical ideas portrayed in cloth pictures will cover a wide range: activities in which they are involved (getting on the school bus); things they see around them (radio towers across the street from the school); stories they have read (*Snow White and the Seven Dwarfs*); things they have read about (crop dusting from airplanes); things they imagine—from clowns to haunted houses!

The unusualness of the materials will make the lesson an exciting one, and the finished pictures will have an intriguing effect that you can't get any other way. Before displaying them, mount them on a piece of heavy cardboard to keep them flat.

Make It Easy—for Yourself!

1. Have the burlap cut, and ready to pass out before the lesson begins. A variety of colors for children to choose from will add interest to the work and more appeal to the finished products.
2. Tear the cloth—plain and printed percale—into small pieces of about 6 x 9 inches.
3. Separate the different kinds of materials into individual piles. Spot some of each in different sections of the room. Assign parts of the class to each area so as to make less congestion at any one place as children return to get more materials.

Variations

1. Use seasonal or holiday motifs in a cloth picture.
2. Make a large wall-hanging or mural. Let it become a group or entire class project.

Variation for Lower Grades

Use cloth to make only one or two important parts of the picture. Paste the cloth onto 12 x 18 manila or white drawing paper. Use tempera paint (or crayon) to complete the rest of the picture.

Variations for Higher Grades

1. Begin the picture as previously described. Then add details by doing some stitchery with yarn or embroidery cotton. Large eye tapestry or crewel needles will be needed if stitching with yarn.
2. Create a *collage* with various kinds of materials appliqued to burlap. Add stitchery of yarn or embroidery cotton if desired.

Lesson Two: Let's Go Shopping!

CLOTHES

Everybody likes to have new clothes. A whole new Easter outfit is just wonderful, but even a pretty new dress or a flashy new sport shirt gives you a big lift. Children enjoy it, too, but they don't always have a chance to pick their own clothes. Today let's go shopping!

Get together an assortment of materials: prints, plaids, solid colors, stripes, any kind you can get your hands on. Have them cut or torn in moderately small pieces—somewhere near 6 x 9 will be easy to handle. Make it exciting by pretending these are all in a store as you make a pile of each different kind on a table.

Talk about going shopping for new clothes. Wouldn't it be fun to go all by yourself and pick out anything you like? If you could

141

buy just one thing, what would you like? Would you buy a shirt or a pair of trousers or a jacket? Would you buy a blouse or a skirt or a party dress? Let the children talk about what they would like to have the most.

Then as one group at a time visits the store—not to overcrowd it, of course—pass out scissors. Let the children begin making their new clothes. Perhaps they can think of some way to pleat the skirt, or gather the waist, or make a crease in the new trousers, or make real pockets on the shirt. Clothes aren't just flat pieces of cloth, you know.

But new clothes aren't any good unless you wear them! Pass out 12 x 18 manila paper and crayons so that the children can draw themselves and model those pretty new things. Also use crayons to draw any of the clothes that aren't brand new. Encourage the children to make themselves and their new clothes as big as they can. Paste on the new clothes, leaving them free from the paper wherever possible in order to create a three-dimensional effect.

Have a table covered with newspaper and equipped with easel brushes and black paint. Some of the children will want to use the paint to outline the crayon and cloth picture of themselves.

The children will love to go shopping. They'll be mighty proud of themselves, too, almost feeling as though they *do* have new dresses or skirts or trousers.

Make It Easy—for Yourself!

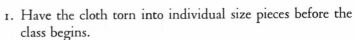

1. Have the cloth torn into individual size pieces before the class begins.
2. Have a separate area for the painting. If space is severely limited, the painting area may replace the "store" area after each child has chosen his material.
3. With several kinds of materials being used at one time— paper, cloth, paste, scissors, crayons—it is a help for the teacher to collect some of the materials after they have been used. For example, as the teacher walks about the room she could collect the scissors after a child has finished with them. Similarly, she could collect the paste once the child begins with the crayons. This solves some of the clean-up problem at the end of the lesson and also enables the child to have more work space.

4. No pencils. Cut the cloth and use the crayons without previous pencil drawing.

Variation

Use crayons and cloth to make other people: father, mother, policeman, clown.

Variation for Lower Grades

Use paper instead of cloth for the new clothes. Gift wrapping paper would make an interesting variety to take the place of cloth. Use paint or crayon for the rest of the person.

Variation for Upper Grade

Let each child have several pieces of cloth to make all the clothes with material. Discuss the combination of plain and printed materials.

Lesson Three: As Different As Can Be!

STITCHERY

WE'RE GOING TO BE DIFFERENT TODAY! WE WON'T use paper—we'll use cloth. We won't use paint or crayon—we'll use felt or yarn. We won't use paint brushes—we'll use needles. We'll be as different as can be!

So gather together all the materials you will need. Burlap makes a fine background for a stitchery picture—its course, rough texture is pleasing to look at as well as easy to use. Of course you'll want needles with eyes large enough to use with yarn. In addition, have an assortment of ma-

144

terials: cloth (plain and print), felt, cotton roving, yarn, embroidery cotton.

Talk about what you could do with each of these things. The cloth and the felt you would have to applique to the burlap. They could be cut into any kinds of shapes and attached to form solid areas—big, middle-size, or little areas. The roving, too, would have to be appliqued on, but it could be used to create thick lines instead of shapes. And the yarn and embroidery cotton? Why, that can be sewn right into the burlap. You can do all kinds of things with that!

Let's investigate some of the things you can do with yarn or embroidery cotton. Have a small piece of scrap burlap on which you can explore some of the possibilities. Just stitching in and out of the threads of the burlap—almost like weaving—is one easy way to begin. Try some variations of just this one technique: in and out of every other thread, or under one and over two, or under two and over three, or any other repeat pattern you like. Try several. Stretch them out in a long line or repeat them close together so that they form an almost solid mass.

Then try some other things. How about crossing one stitch over another—a cross stitch! Learn how to make a chain stitch—or group them together to form a flower. Try other simple stitches that you know. (Or find directions for some easy embroidery stitches.) Fill the whole piece of practice burlap with as many kinds of stitches as you can think of.

Now let's plan a stitchery picture. Do you want to cut out shapes to applique onto the burlap? Or would you rather begin with a piece of cotton roving creating an interesting line design? Whichever way you decide to begin, choose your color carefully. Lay the lines or the shapes on the burlap background. Move them about until you are pleased. Then fasten them down with any of the stitches you have experimented with on your practice piece.

There! That's a good beginning! Do you want to add more solid shapes to those empty areas, perhaps overlapping some? Or would you rather use yarn or embroidery cotton to create an interesting line or area? Repeat some of the shapes over and over again, varying the size and placement in the picture. Repeat colors to unify and balance the picture.

Take your time—you won't finish it all in one lesson. But who's in a hurry, anyway! Stitchery pictures grow slowly, but they're so much fun to do. Stapled to a piece of drawing paper to hold them flat, they'll make a display that's as different as can be!

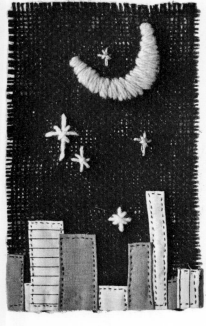

Make It Easy—for Yourself!

1. Have a variety of colored burlap cut to approximately 12 x 18.

2. Have other materials where they are easily available so that children may see the colors and types of materials from which they may choose (plain or printed fabric, roving, yarn, embroidery cotton).

3. Discuss the importance of contrast in color, texture, size. Emphasize basic elements of composition: balance, center of interest, movement, space.

4. Have large-eye needles (tapestry or crewel) suitable for use with yarn.

5. Demonstrate how to thread a needle with yarn and let each child try it. (Holding a needle horizontally between the thumb and forefinger, stretch the yarn over the side of the needle leaving one end about five or six inches long. Pull the needle out so that you are tightly holding a folded piece of yarn. This way there are no fuzzy edges to the yarn, and the eye of the needle may be placed over it and eased down gently until the folded edge of the yarn is through the eye of the needle. It is simple to thread yarn into a needle if done this way. (Don't get the yarn wet—don't put it in your mouth as you might do with thread.)

6. After each child is able to thread a needle, give him a scrap of burlap on which to practice simple stitches. Encourage him to repeat each kind of stitch several times. Even the scrap of burlap may result in an interesting stitchery design.

7. As soon as a child has demonstrated his ability to design with a needle and yarn, let him choose his burlap and one or more materials with which to begin his picture.

8. Encourage each child to plan the large areas of his picture first.

9. Warn the children not to pull their stitches too tight as this would pucker the fabric.

10. Frequently encourage each child to hold his picture as far away from him as possible in order to get a better view of his work as it progresses.

11. Don't stop too soon. Fill some areas solid with plain stitches, cross stitch, French knots, chain stitch. Repeat some motifs, varying size, color, placement.
12. It will take several art lessons to complete this project. Don't try to hurry it.

Variations

1. Make a realistic picture. Use a combination of fabric and yarn, roving, embroidery cotton for solid areas and line effects. Make it a landscape, a seascape, a still life—any kind of realistic picture you might make with cut paper or with paint.
2. Use only embroidery cotton to create a simpler type of picture.

Variations for Lower Grades

1. Make a simple fabric picture of "My House" or "Me." Use an overcasting stitch to sew it to a burlap (or other fabric) background. Place the emphasis on the picture rather than the stitchery. You may need to thread the needles for some of the children who have less manual coordination.
2. Cut an animal from printed fabric. Sew it to a fabric background, leaving a small opening at one edge. Stuff the animal with a little bit of cotton batting to make it slightly three-dimensional. Finish sewing to close the opening.

Lesson Four: Our Heads Are Full of Cotton

FABRIC PUPPETS

MY NAME IS BOZO—I'M A CLOWN! MY NAME is Annabelle—I'm the queen! My name is Hugo—I'm the king! We are colorful, we are lots of fun, and we can be clever, too—even though our heads are full of cotton! Boys and girls love us! We are good for them, too, for we can help them to learn, to express themselves, and to be creative. Anyone can make us for all you need are needles and thread, fabric scraps, cotton batting, a little cardboard, and lots of imagination. Here's how.

Take a little piece of thin cardboard, wide enough to wrap around your index finger and about twice as long. Either paste it closed or wrap it with a rubber band. The top half of the resulting cylinder will be the center part of a head. Wrap a piece of cotton batting around the upper part of the cardboard tube. The amount of cotton depends upon the size you want the head to be. Next take a piece of plain fabric—muslin is good—about twelve inches long and six inches wide. Wrap the fabric snugly around the cotton batting, leaving an inch to an inch and a half of the cloth at the bottom and the rest above the cotton batting. Fold back the end of the fabric to hide the raw edge, and stitch it with a simple running stitch, catching the cotton underneath whenever possible. Next use a double thread (for strength) to sew a running stitch around the bottom edge of the fabric. Gather it to tighten the cloth around the cardboard cylinder. The excess fabric that is on top fold toward the center of the head and stitch it down, catching the cotton to hold it in place. You now have a cotton batting stuffed head with a seam down one side.

Imaginations can run wild as these cotton heads take on character and meaning. Before adding features, make sure that the seam is turned toward the back of the head, leaving a smooth area for the face. Add eyes, nose, mouth, hair. Buttons or colored paper may be pasted on the face. Felt is also ideal, for it has no raw edges and can be either pasted or sewed to the face. Yarn makes fine hair. Other combinations of scraps and treasures may be used.

Clothes for puppets can be made in several ways. Take a large piece of fabric, simply drape it over your hand, and put your index finger into the cylinder. You then have a cape-like garment. Or a cloak may also be made in the form of a "T" with openings for neck and arms. This will give a more realistic garment as well as giving the puppet greater freedom of movement. Another way of making clothes is to cut two holes about four inches apart near the center of a piece of fabric. The thumb and middle finger when put through these holes become arms. The index finger covered with fabric is put into the cylinder—the neck of the puppet.

The love of pretending becomes evident as the puppets take on unique child-like personalities, full of enthusiasm and originality. Try it and have your own original and creative theatrical venture—with heads that are full of cotton!

Make It Easy—for Yourself!

1. Have the fabric pieces for the heads pre-cut, with matching thread available.

2. Have the cotton batting torn apart in appropriate lengths. This can be done by the teacher before the lesson or by the children as part of the lesson.
3. Have a wide assortment of materials available. Have them arranged so that each child may make his own selection.
4. Divide the project into as many lessons as you think necessary, depending upon the length of time available for an art lesson.
5. Stress good workmanship in stitching.
6. Demonstrate the sewing part of the lesson and, if possible, make a puppet as an illustration.
7. Have each child choose a character or personality before he begins so that he will be able to create a particular feeling in his finished puppet.

Variations for Lower Grades

1. Start with a small styrofoam ball. Dig out a hole for the index finger. Facial features can be made from cut paper pinned onto the ball—or from buttons, yarn, jewelry, rick-rack, or any other inspirational material. Costumes may be made as described in the above lesson.
2. Start with a paper plate stapled to a cardboard stick. Make a face (with paper or paint) and decorate the head with fabric hats, hair, ribbons, or caps. Gather a two foot width of fabric with a running stitch along one end. Wrap it around the cardboard stick near the plate to conceal the manipulator's arm. This costume may also be decorated with paper, jewelry, and other treasures.

OBJECTIVES

1. To use fabric in a new and creative way.

2. To discover that body can be given to a limp material so that it may be used three-dimensionally.

3. To encourage originality in three-dimensional art.

4. To use the pattern and texture of fabric as an important part of a composition.

(For grades 5 and 6)

Lesson Five: Let's Fabricate!

FABRIC IN BAS RELIEF

WHEN YOU FABRICATE A STORY, YOU MAY BE stretching the truth. But when you fabricate a picture, you use art media in a new and different way. The beauty of fabrics is in their colors, patterns, and textures. How would you like to use them to create a bas relief picture that is outstanding in its crispness and originality? Okay, then let's fabricate a picture!

We have two problems to solve. It is difficult to use fabric in a picture of any kind because of raw edges which tend to ravel and get ragged. It is also difficult to create a relief picture with fabric because of its lack of body. Here's the solution. Select the fabric you'd like to use—it can be stripes, dots, patterns, or anything that catches your eye—and cut it down to a piece small enough to be easily handled. Take a piece of light-weight cardboard—oaktag is fine—and coat it with paste. Apply the fabric over it and press it down with your hand until the wrinkles are gone.

Select a neutral or contrasting color of construction paper. This will be the base and background for your bas relief picture. Cut out the fabric coated cardboard in the shapes that will comprise your picture. For example, you may cut individual petals for a flower, or the hull of a boat, or the body of a swan, or the head of an animal. The fabric has a tendency to curl, and this can be used to advantage, as you will see.

Our fabric now has body, so we want to make sure that our picture is not flat or two-dimensional. Let's describe making a flower. After a number of petals are cut out, roll them around your finger so that they have a slight curl. Apply paste on the cardboard side of the petal, putting it only at the end which will be pasted onto the construction paper. You now have a rhythmic, flowing petal attached at one end, with the other end free and standing up from the surface. Continue placing the petals on the construction paper in a circular arrangement so that they radiate out from a center point. Smaller petals may be cut and overlapped on the larger ones for a fuller, lush blossom. Cut out larger leaves from another fabric (pasted to the cardboard), curl it, paste one end, and slip it under the relief flower.

Any other subject matter can be made in this bas relief technique. A flat piece of fabric board can be made to stand up from the surface by pasting both ends and pushing toward the center—or by curling, folding, or shaping.

The results are enchanting, as the patterns and colors are interpreted in this crisp relief form. Your composition looks as if you spent hours painting and drawing designs for your picture—but we know the truth, don't we?

Make It Easy—for Yourself!

1. Have a variety of print and plain fabric torn into pieces small enough to be easy to handle (somewhere near 6 x 9 would be appropriate). Have it arranged so that each child may make his own selections.
2. Have enough oaktag (or similar weight paper) cut about the same size as the cloth so that each person may have several pieces.

3. Apply paste to the oaktag rapidly so that no part of it dries before the fabric is placed on top of it.

4. No pencils! Pencil lines detract from the beauty of the finished product—and tend to make things too small and detailed.

Variations

1. Vary the theme of your fabricated pictures: still life, imaginary bugs, animals, people.

2. Make only a part of your picture with bas relief fabric. Make the background of a landscape or seascape with paint or cut paper.

TRANSPARENT

8.

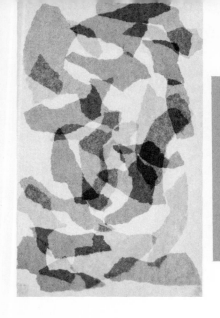

OBJECTIVES

1. **To use familiar materials in a new and exciting way.**

2. **To use transparent material to demonstrate how colors are affected by other colors—thereby enriching the color sense and experience of young people.**

3. **To introduce the idea of overlapping parts of a picture.**

(For K through grade 2, adapted to grades 3 through 6)

CHAPTER **8** *Transparent Materials*

Lesson One: Sandwiches

WAX PAPER TRANSPARENCIES

LET'S MAKE SANDWICHES! OH, WE WON'T EAT these sandwiches, they'll be much too pretty for that. We'll just look at them. But they'll be sandwiches just the same. We'll have a top layer and a bottom layer and a filling in between. Now, that's what a sandwich is, isn't it? So let's see how we'll make them.

This is going to be a pretty sandwich and we'll want to see what's inside it. So we'll start with a piece of "bread" that we can see through. This wax paper will be just fine for that. Tear off a long piece about two feet long. Fold it in half, for the top and bottom layer of the sandwich.

Now let's put in the filling. To begin with I'll tear off some of this red (or any other color) tissue paper. I'll make some of the pieces big with ragged edges. Some will be small, and some will be in-between sizes. Some I'll make round and fat, and some I'll make long and thin.

156

Lay them on one half of the folded wax paper, being sure that none of them go all the way to the edge of the paper. Overlap some of them and leave some all by themselves.

When there is enough of one color in the "sandwich," take a second color tissue paper. Tear pieces from it just as you did before. Let them overlap some of the others. Notice the new color they make. Then add a third color. Make them different sizes and shapes, too— big shapes, little shapes, fat shapes, skinny shapes, plain shapes, fancy shapes. Point out new colors that appear—get the children (who are standing in a group around you) to notice and comment about them.

That's a good looking filling, isn't it! Much too good to eat! We'll put the top layer over it (as you again lay the top half of the wax paper over the torn pieces of tissue paper). But a sandwich isn't any good if it falls apart, so we'll have to do something to make this one stay together.

Slide a piece of cardboard under the sandwich and carefully carry it to a place which you have previously prepared as an ironing area. Lay the cardboard and the sandwich on it and then slide out the cardboard. Place another piece of newspaper over the sandwich to protect it, and with a medium hot iron press the whole thing.

What will happen as the hot iron goes over the wax paper? That's right! The wax will melt and stick together! And the tissue paper filling will be right inside it.

Remove the newspaper over the design and hold the finished picture up to the light. See, there it is—a sandwich picture!—too pretty to eat but nice to look at.

Let each child have a piece of wax paper and a choice of colored tissue paper. After the tissue paper has been torn and the filling made, let the children take turns bringing their sandwich to the ironing area. (Carry them on the cardboard to keep them from falling apart.) A quick pressing with a medium hot iron and you'll be ready to display the finished transparent pictures. When they're taped to the glass, the windows will come alive with color—sandwiches too pretty to eat but fascinating to look at.

Make It Easy—for Yourself!

1. Have a variety of colored tissue paper cut to approximately 4 x 6. Use colors as bright as possible.

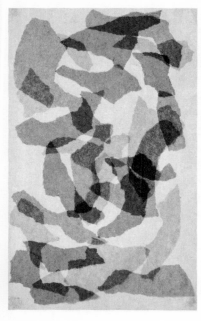

2. Tear the wax paper into pieces about two feet long. With a kindergarten class you may want to have the wax paper folded in half before giving it to the children.
3. Have a piece of cardboard to be shared by each group of several children.
4. Prepare an ironing area by having a fairly thick pile of newspaper—so that the heat won't penetrate to the surface of the table or desk.
5. Have enough extra pieces of newspaper at the ironing area so that a fresh piece will always be available to place on top of the sandwich.
6. Have children print their names on small pieces of paper which can be inserted near the edge of the sandwich. This can be ironed into the picture for easy identification.
7. Carefully supervise the ironing to be certain that the hot iron is used correctly.
8. Have masking tape (or other adhesive) available so that finished transparencies may be immediately displayed at the windows.

Variations

1. Use paper—tissue or construction—to cut out or tear objects (or just interesting shapes). Scrape off bits of old wax crayons and let them drop onto the wax paper. Iron as before to seal the parts together. The bits of wax crayon will melt and blend together to add more color and interest to the transparency.
2. Place natural materials (leaves, grasses, ferns that have been dried and pressed) between sheets of wax paper. Bits of wax crayon may be added for extra interest. Press as before.

Variations for Higher Grades

1. Use paper—tissue or construction—to cut out objects that will form a realistic picture. Scrape off bits of old wax crayons to suggest background areas (for example, water in a seascape), or just to add color interest.

2. Use string (or yarn) to "draw" the basic outline of a picture. Add color—either bits of crayons or tiny bits of tissue paper—to fill in between the outline areas. Press in the usual way.

3. Make a long, narrow transparency. Start with a piece of wax paper about 18 to 24 inches long. Fold it the narrow way to make a long, thin picture. Complete in any of the ways previously described.

4. Draw a simple outline shape on 12 x 18 manila paper. Avoid intricate details and keep all areas wide. Place a sheet of wax paper over the design and trace it onto the wax paper. This may be done by pressing heavily with the point of a pencil. Within the traced shape place cut or torn pieces of colored tissue paper or cellophane. Overlap them to create interesting colors and shapes. Scrape pieces of old crayons over the design to give the finished picture body as well as rich color. Place another piece of wax paper over the whole thing and press it with a warm iron. The traced line which was etched into the wax paper will still show. Cut out on these lines. Punch a hole in the top so that the finished transparency can be suspended when it is displayed.

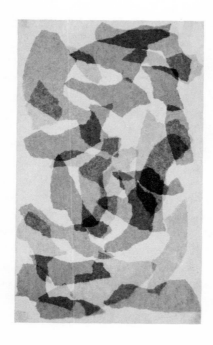

Lesson Two: Spin the Wheel of Color

CELLOPHANE COLOR CYLINDERS

IT'S TIME TO START SPINNING THE WHEELS OF imagination and learning about color. Let's try something that will be more exciting and meaningful than the standard two-dimensional color wheel. Let's create a three-dimensional cylinder which, as it revolves, dramatically shows the blending and mixing of colors. It's easy to make and all you need is construction paper; red, yellow, and blue cellophane; scissors; and glue.

First let's take a piece of 9 x 12 construction paper (black is best) and cut it to make an attractive free-form shape. We shouldn't cut too much of it away, or it will be too small. Next we cut out three smaller free-form shapes within our larger solid shape, making sure we don't cut through to the edge of the original shape. It is important to leave at least three-quarters of an inch between each cut-out

160

and the outside edge of the paper. We now have a free-form shape with three other free-form shapes cut out of it.

Around any one of the smaller shapes, apply glue, and on top of that put down one color of cellophane. Also do this with the other two shapes until you have three colored windows, one each of red, yellow, and blue cellophane. The cellophane should be neatly trimmed around each shape after it is firmly attached. Make sure that each child works on only one side of the construction paper.

Now all we have to do is to roll up our design into a lantern-like cylinder and paste the edges together where they overlap. Of course, the glued side of the wheel is now on the inside of our cylinder. If you attach a black thread from the top of the cylinder, and let it revolve, the light coming through the primary colors will change them into the secondary colors. Not only the colors will change, but new shapes will appear as well. The class will be delighted as the secondary colors of green, orange, and violet seem to magically appear within the spinning cylinder.

Make It Easy—for Yourself!

1. Be sure there is at least three-quarters of an inch of construction paper around any cut out part.
2. Cover all work areas with newspaper so that the glue will not get on the furiture. (Glue may remove the finish from wood surfaces.)
3. Be sure to use glue to adhere the cellophane to the construction paper, as paste will not hold to cellophane.
4. Give each child a piece of red, yellow, and blue cellophane at the beginning of the work period.
5. After the construction paper frames have been made, the teacher may collect the scraps. This will provide more work area, and will make for an easier cleanup.
6. No pencils! Cut the free-form shapes without any preliminary drawing.

Variations

1. Cut out geometric shapes from cellophane of each of the

primary colors. Glue them to clear cellophane which has been attached to construction paper frames. Overlap the shapes so that the secondary colors appear and so that new shapes are created.

2. Fold a piece of 12 x 18 black construction paper in thirds so that each section will be about 6 x 12. Cut any shape (holiday or seasonal motifs may be used) from each of the three vertical sections. The shapes may be all the same or all different, but related in subject matter (for example: spring—birds, flowers, bugs, trees, butterflies). Cover each shape with a primary color cellophane. Bring the two open edges together and staple near the edges. Also staple at the top and bottom of each fold to give the triangular shape more strength. Display either as a stationary object or as a mobile.

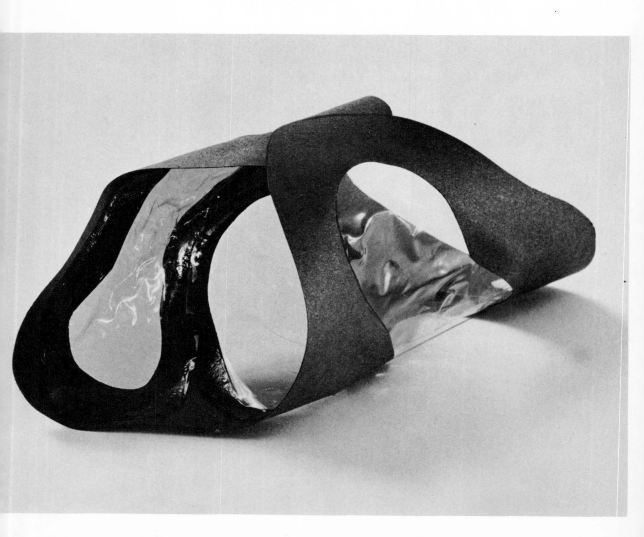

OBJECTIVES

1. To investigate and appreciate the color and translucent beauty of tissue paper.

2. To use drawing as a basis for a unique project.

3. To develop the use of simple line in a composition.

(For grades 5 and 6)

Lesson Three: Captured!

CRUMPLED TISSUE PAPER

COLORED TISSUE PAPER IS BEAUTIFUL, BUT IT FRUS-trates me! In piles the colors are extremely vivid, but with one sheet alone the color becomes pale and washed out. Yet, when I hold it up to the light, although it's pale, it has a delicately pleasing glow. How can I capture both these qualities—the vivid color and the translucent glow? I think I've got it! I'll capture them—I mean literally *capture* them!

On a piece of 9 x 12 manila paper, sketch a picture you'd like to make. Draw one object—a vase of flowers, a face, a cat—and keep it simple and fairly large with little or no detail. Draw with crayons to help keep it simple. On top of the manila paper place a piece of wax paper. Trace the shape by pressing with the point of a pencil. We are going to reproduce the drawing with crumpled tissue paper, so choose the appropriate colors.

Tear off a strip of tissue paper about three inches wide. Twist or crumple the tissue paper until you get a narrow, long piece.

Apply paste or glue to the wax paper, covering the object drawn on the manila paper and traced on the wax paper. Place the long narrow strip of tissue paper on the pasted area of the wax paper to anchor it. When we crumple the tissue paper we notice that the vivid color found in the pile returns as the paper overlaps itself. Continue to crumple tissue paper and apply to pasted areas until the whole drawing is reconstructed. The crumpled paper may be large and loose for long lines or tight and narrow to outline smaller shapes.

When the picture is completed, cover it with another piece of wax paper. With a warm iron press around the outside of the picture. This will fuse the two layers of wax paper together, capturing our tissue picture.

Trim around the picture following its general outline, leaving at least an inch of wax paper as a border. We must not cut off too much of the wax paper or our picture will lose its strength and our tissue paper will escape!

Punch a hole at the top of the wax paper and suspend the picture in front of a window or a light and enjoy the results! We now see the light coming through the vivid colors of the crumpled tissue paper. The two qualities—color and translucency—are indeed captured!

Make It Easy—for Yourself!

1. Use crayons rather than pencils to draw object on manila paper. This tends to make the drawing larger with less detail.
2. If you use glue, be sure to cover all work areas with newspaper. (Glue may lift the finish if it gets on furniture.)
3. Use as bright colors of tissue paper as possible. Have a wide range of colors from which to choose.
4. Have the sheets of tissue paper cut in quarters (or even smaller) to make them easier to handle. Arrange piles of each color in two or more parts of the room so that there will never be too many children choosing colors from one place at any time.
5. Have an ironing area where children may press to seal the edges of their picture when they are ready for that part of

the lesson. A thick pad of newspapers makes a good ironing board.

Variations

1. Use a holiday or seasonal theme with appropriate colors and objects.
2. Have the class work in groups, each group making an object with a central theme. Arrange these objects as a mobile on a coat hanger structure.
3. Make free-form shapes filled with the crumpled tissue paper. These may also be used on a mobile.

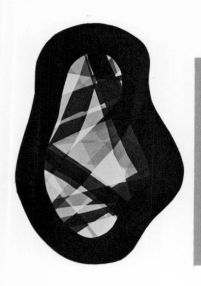

Lesson Four: Criss-Cross Equals—Color!

CELLOPHANE STRIPS

EVERYONE LOVES COLOR, AND IT BECOMES EVEN more exciting when you can actually manipulate, change, and create *new* colors. Sound technical? Involved? Or messy? Well—believe it or not—it's perhaps one of the easiest lessons you can teach and one of the most rewarding. All you do is criss-cross and—color comes alive!

Using two sheets of black 9 x 12 construction paper, hold them together and cut out a free-form shape. Still holding them together, cut out the center of the shape, leaving at least a three-quarter inch strip as a border. You now have two identical free-form doughnut shapes. Put one shape aside, and take three pieces of cellophane, one each of the three primary colors; red, yellow, and blue. Cut out strips of cellophane, long enough that the ends can reach both sides of the doughnut.

166

Fasten the cellophane strips to the black paper with glue—only a tiny drop is needed. The cellophane strip is attached to both sides of the free form, spanning the cut-out opening. Make sure the glue is placed only on the construction paper so that none will show through the opening. Don't let the cellophane extend beyond the construction paper. Overlap the strips until the entire opening is covered by brilliant colors, overlapping to create many, many new shapes and colors.

Put a thin line of glue around the shape, and top the design with the other identical paper shape. Your glowing design is now finished. It is attractive from both sides, so you may put a small hole in one end and suspend it from the ceiling, the light fixtures, or in front of the windows.

The array of color is breathtaking as the three primary colors mix and make the secondary colors—green, orange, and violet. There is a variety of shades of colors and shapes caused by overlapping the cellophane strips. In this case, criss-cross equals—color!

Make It Easy—for Yourself!

1. Be sure the frame is at least ¾ of an inch all the way around to prevent it from breaking.
2. Cover all work areas with newspaper so that the glue will not get on the furniture. (Glue may remove the finish from wood surfaces.)
3. Give each child a strip of red, yellow, and blue cellophane as well as two pieces of 9 x 12 black construction paper.
4. After the construction paper frames have been made, the teacher may collect the scraps. This will provide more working area as well as making for an easier clean-up.
5. Stress the importance of cutting cellophane strips long enough to reach all the way across the cut-out section, from one edge of the frame to the other.
6. Overlap all cellophane strips to create a variety of new colors and shapes.

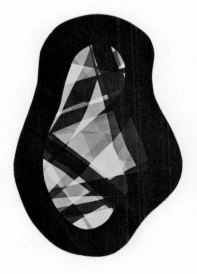

Variations

1. Fold the construction paper in half and cut out a realistic

shape: vase, bottle, flower, fish, or any other object. Cut out the inside and proceed as described.

2. Use as a holiday lesson, cutting out motifs such as bells, candles, Christmas trees, rabbits, Easter eggs, valentines. Suspend them from a coat hanger armature to make a holiday mobile.

Variations for Lower Grades

1. Cut only one paper frame. Use pre-cut strips, criss-crossing them as previously described. Display finished pictures in windows.
2. Cut out the center of the construction paper in a free-form shape and paste tissue paper strips to it.
3. Cut out frames and use construction paper strips for a non-objective, non-transparent design.

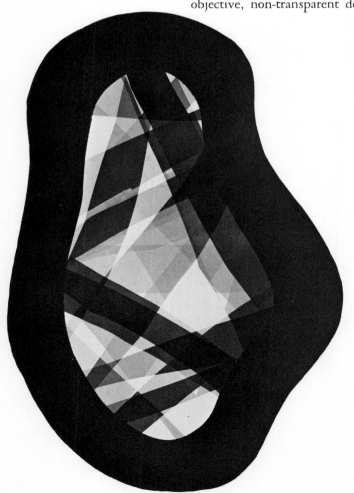

Lesson Five: The Mystery of Light

TISSUE AND CONSTRUCTION PAPER

THE BEAUTY OF LIGHT IS ALWAYS A FASCINATING mystery. Let's create a beautiful illusion with colored tissue paper, black construction paper, and light—sun or artificial light. The illusion is one of distance with a subtle blending of colors.

We begin by taking a piece of 9 x 12 black construction paper, folding it in half and cutting out the center, leaving at least an inch border. Begin cutting on the folded edge, continue around, and come out on the same folded edge. When the paper is opened it becomes a frame on which will be built our picture. The inside of the frame may be cut straight for a plain, uniform border, or it may be cut in a pattern (scallops, points, waves) to create a more designed edge.

Now let's begin our picture. The subject matter is up to the artist—it can be almost anything. Let's try an outdoor scene so that we can show the illusion of distance. Upon our frame we attach the objects which will be our center of interest. We do this by pasting

169

cut-out shapes to the bottom of our frame. Most of the shape is above the frame, showing through the opening. In our model we will use a house, trees, and perhaps a lamp post. Our cut-out village scene can be done in colored construction paper. Or, better yet, let's use the piece of black construction paper we cut out when we made our frame.

After the objects in our picture have been pasted to our frame, we place a light color of tissue paper on top of the scene. We do this by putting paste on our frame and placing the tissue paper on top. You may think that this hides our scene and ruins our picture, but actually we are working on the wrong side of our picture, for when we turn it over, we see our scene in front of a beautiful translucent color. Wait! We're not finished yet! The fun has only begun.

Behind our village scene we can place mountains or hills, overlapping as many colors as are available. Shades of green and yellow may be overlapped for hills that are close, while blues and purples make fine mountains in the distance. Yellows and oranges will create an interesting sunset. A little imagination can create many more startling effects. We must always remember to work on the wrong side of our picture. Our tissue paper backing creates an illusion of depth and distance. Because of this, it is best to begin overlapping the tissue paper to show those things which are closer before showing parts which are farther back in the picture. By overlapping the many colors of tissue paper, we can create new shapes and colors as well as the illusion of depth.

Tissue shapes should be long enough so they may be attached on the sides of the frame, so that paste will not be seen in the transparent part of the picture. If smaller parts of tissue paper are used, care should be taken not to use too much paste, so that it also will not show in the finished picture. Our original construction paper cut-outs may need a dab of paste behind them to hold them to our backing of tissue paper.

When we turn our picture over and hold it up to the light, we have a beautiful scene with definite solid shapes in the foreground and a delicate blending of colors forming the background. Once again we have seen the mystery of light as it filters through the tissue paper and creates new shapes, colors, and an illusion of depth and beauty.

Make It Easy—for Yourself!

1. Pre-cut tissue to 9 x 12 rectangles.

2. Arrange tissue paper in color stacks so that the children may choose the colors they want to use.
3. Have children share colors so as not to cut into so many pieces.
4. Distribute paste on small pieces of scrap paper.
5. Press finished pictures under weights over night to prevent curling.

Variations

1. Make a cut-out picture with construction paper on white drawing paper. Top the picture with a piece of colored tissue plus a frame.
2. Paste cut-out construction paper picture on top of a piece of tissue paper. Overlap it with another piece of tissue paper and add a construction paper frame.
3. Make a cut-out picture or design of tissue paper on top of tissue paper, overlapping pieces as much as possible. Then add a frame.

hree

nensional

9.

CHAPTER **9** *Three-Dimensional Materials*

Lesson One: Quick and Easy

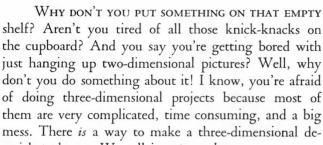

STRIP SCULPTURE

Why don't you put something on that empty shelf? Aren't you tired of all those knick-knacks on the cupboard? And you say you're getting bored with just hanging up two-dimensional pictures? Well, why don't you do something about it! I know, you're afraid of doing three-dimensional projects because most of them are very complicated, time consuming, and a big mess. There *is* a way to make a three-dimensional design which is quick and easy. We call it *strip sculpture*.

Choose three colors of 9 x 12 construction paper. Cut one into a rhythmic free-form shape. This will become a base or foundation upon which our sculpture will be built. Cut the other two pieces into strips of varying sizes (both width and length). Fold back toward the middle of the strip about a quarter of an inch at each end. Apply paste to the folded sections and secure one end to the base paper. The other end, when pushed toward the secured end, causes the strip to arch. Fasten down the other end, making an arch of your own choosing. From this point on you can do almost anything with these strips. One end can be fastened on the existing arch with the other on the base. The strips can be folded or coiled and attached to one another, placed independently, or overlapped.

You can create wonderful and exciting constructions just with the interplay of the colored strips. These sculptures may become tall and graceful, short and solid, or whimsical in their appearance. Variety in the width and length of strips is very important. Try to keep the sculptures simple and uncluttered, or they will grow and grow and grow. Concentrate on simple, clean curves with only a touch of folded and curly strips.

The finished product, although abstract, may often resemble a realistic object, and it is great fun to try and see what our imaginations can find. This three-dimensional sculpture—height, width, and depth—is certainly quick and easy.

Make It Easy—for Yourself!

1. Arrange 9 x 12 construction paper in piles, according to color, in two different areas of the room. Let children take turns selecting their choices of colors. By having two areas for the paper, the selection can be done more rapidly and without confusion.

2. Give out a small piece of newspaper so that all pasting can be done on that.

3. No pencils! Cut without any preliminary drawing.

4. Cut very little from the paper that is to be the base—only enough to make an interesting free-form shape.

5. Distribute small amounts of paste on scrap paper to each child.

6. Encourage children to turn their constructions as they work on them so that they may see them from all angles.

7. Finished designs may be displayed on a flat, horizontal surface, or may be tacked to a bulletin board—with the base flat against the bulletin.

Variations

1. Make a realistic object using strips as the basic unit of construction.
2. Make futuristic buildings, space stations, rockets, or other highly imaginative or imaginary objects.
3. Use strips to make an abstract shape with no base at all. These may then be suspended or made to stand by themselves.

Variation for Lower Grades

Use pre-cut strips and a paper plate for the base. Build the construction with the strips, not introducing other paper sculpture techniques. Limit the number of strips and keep them fairly wide.

Lesson Two: Just a Pet

CONSTRUCTION PAPER STUFFED ANIMALS

EVERY LITTLE GIRL AND BOY LOVES AN ANIMAL, and a stuffed toy animal is the next best thing to a real one. It doesn't have to be an elaborate one—just a pet that can be picked up. So let's make a simple one out of a couple of pieces of paper.

Have some paints ready (or even crayons, if you prefer). Then talk to the class about animals they like. If you could have any kind of animal, what kind would you want? Would he be a regular pet like a cat or a dog—or perhaps a rabbit or a horse? Or what *would* you like? Get the children to talk about their favorite animals.

Then suggest that they each make an animal, whatever kind of pet each would most like to have. But, of course, he has to be a strong animal—so make him big. He isn't going to be just a picture of a cat or a rabbit or an elephant—he's going to be a *real* one. He'll be cut out of two pieces of paper and stuffed, so stress the importance of making the legs thick, thick enough to stuff. Make the ears and tail big, too, so that they won't tear off when they're cut out. Make everything big, BIG, B-I-G!

Pass out 12 x 18 manila or white drawing paper (or 18 x 24, if you prefer) and begin the painting or crayon drawing of the favorite animal. Be sure it's big! Better get those skinny little legs fatter so they won't break off. An animal with a broken leg wouldn't be much good. That's better, keep them big and thick.

When the painting or drawing is finished, carefully cut it out. But that's still only a picture. Another animal just like it has to be made. Then we can put them together and stuff them to make a real animal. So on another paper the same size make another animal —but be sure he's going in the opposite direction. Just turn the first one upside down on the new paper and trace it with a crayon. Then complete it with paint or crayon to look like the first picture. Cut it out and place the two parts together, the finished sides out.

The teacher may then staple the parts together, leaving one open space big enough that small pieces of crumpled newspaper may be put inside. When the animal has "eaten" enough newspaper to be plump and soft, staple the open section. And *presto!* there is a real animal instead of just a picture!

The children will love them and promptly give them individual names. Display them—for as long, that is, as you can keep those little hands off their special pets.

Make It Easy—for Yourself!

1. Stress the importance of making all the parts thick. Some space will be taken up with the staples and enough needs to be left so that small pieces of crumpled newspaper can be stuffed into it.

2. Be sure the first animal shape is turned over before it is traced on the second sheet of paper, to be painted or finished with crayons. This will make the two sides of the animal.

3. Staple the two sides together at frequent intervals to strengthen the animal and to keep the newspaper stuffing inside. Small pieces of torn and crumpled newspaper can then be inserted into the animal through one section which has been left open. Finally, close that section with one or two staples.

4. Collect materials as the children finish with them. This makes for an orderly work and clean-up time and also permits more work area free from unnecessary materials. For example, collect the scissors and scraps of paper before distributing newspaper for stuffing.

Variations

1. Make three-dimensional figures of people: themselves, mother, father, friend.
2. Illustrate characters in a story: people, animals, even important objects. Use them to make a three-dimensional mural, as puppets, or just as 3-D illustrations.

Variations for Higher Grades

1. Make animals or people out of cloth and sew the parts together. Stuff with cotton batting.
2. Make only one side of the animals, people, or objects. Cut them from printed cloth. Applique them to large pieces of burlap or other plain pieces of cloth. Stuff slightly with cotton batting to create a 3-D effect.
3. Have the whole class work on one large piece of cloth so as to make a mural. Applique all large objects onto the mural background. Stuff them slightly to give a three-dimensional effect. Add yarn or roving stitchery to complete the scene.

Lesson Three: Spice to the Classroom

TISSUE PAPER MOBILES

HERE'S AN IDEA FOR A FASCINATING ART LESSON that uses a medium which is colorful, new, and exciting to work with. The result has an oriental feeling and is highly decorative, adding just enough spice to the classroom to make it a showplace.

The finished product is a three-dimensional creature made of colored tissue paper, stuffed and decorated with other colors of tissue. When suspended, it becomes aglow with rainbow-like colors as the light shines through it. And it's simple to do!

As as example, let's make an imaginary fish as bright and gay as a sparkling prism! Begin by drawing a basic fish shape on a piece of 12 x 18 paper. Leave off his tail and fins and any details, for this comes later. On top of the pencil drawing, place a piece of colored transparent tissue paper and, with thick paste, follow *just outside* the edge of the pencil outline, making a band of paste a half inch wide. Do not paste all the way around the outline! Make sure you leave at least three inches not pasted, for this will become the opening for stuffing the object.

On top of this tissue paper place another piece of the same color and gently press along the paste band. Now cut out the shape, leaving a half inch margin outside the paste. This is a preliminary trim until the paste is dry. Select light and dark colors for stuffing, keeping in mind that scraps are ideal for this purpose. Tear and crumple pieces of tissue paper and insert them carefully through the unpasted opening. As the paste dries, forming a stiff supporting skeleton, the fish will become easier to handle and can be stuffed more tightly. When the shape is strong enough to support itself, yet not too stuffed as to be non-transparent, trim it to the outside edge of the paste, and seal the opening.

You are now ready for the final touches. The fish needs a beautiful tail, flowing fins, and expressive eyes. Let's begin with his eyes. Cut out a bold pair of eyes either from a very dark tissue, or black construction paper and paste one on each side of its head. You can make him sad, angry, surprised, or happy. Next add a multicolor tail by overlapping several colors of tissue. Make a long flowing tail by combining several pieces of different lengths, or a stiff perky tail by cutting out eliptical shapes, folding them in half for strength, and attaching them on the paste band, the inside fold on the paste edge. Several layers in different sizes can be used here, too. Graceful long fins of different colors and sizes are then attached to both sides of his body. In order to achieve a soft flowing effect, have the fin shapes pointing up toward the top of the body, and apply paste to the bottom edge. When the fish is suspended, the fins will roll gently down, making a graceful movement of their own.

Find a good balance point on the top side of the fish, punch a hole through the hardened paste margin, and suspend him by a thread. He is now finished and ready to add color and delight to your room.

This lesson need not be limited to fish shapes, but can incorporate other animals or ideas. As long as the class understands that simplicity and omission of appendages in the original basic shape are the limiting factors. Birds with long flowing tails and wings, and butterflies with multicolor wings are also good shapes and bright and attractive showpieces to add spice to the classroom.

Make It Easy—for Yourself!

1. Have the class work in small groups of four or five children. This can be done by moving several desks together to create a larger work space.
2. Distribute paste on small pieces of scrap paper or any disposable container, one for each group.
3. After the design has been transferred to the tissue, turn the 12 x 18 paper over to be used as a work surface.
4. Have the class use the scraps from the first trimming for stuffing, sharing with each other.
5. Prepare your own sample to show the class. This will provide strong motivation and show possible results.

Variations

1. Use the same medium in a two-dimensional interpretation, stressing design and overlapping.
2. Create a similar two-dimensional design using a mosaic technique. Overlap pieces to create new colors and shapes.

Lesson Four: No Pandora's Box!

THREE-DIMENSIONAL ABSTRACTS

THIS IS NO PANDORA'S BOX! OH, IT HAS ALL KINDS of things in it—but *wonderful* things. And the surprises won't all come from the box, either. The biggest one of all will be the delightful three-dimensional abstract designs that your class will make.

A box of surprises always carries its own built-in interest appeal. What's in this one, anyway? Well, look at that! Here are some little sticks—some long ones and some short ones. Can you change the shape of them? Not without breaking them, can you. So we'll just leave them as they are.

Let's see now—here's something else. A piece of wire! What can you do with wire that you couldn't do with a stick? Certainly, you

183

can bend it. See, you can make all kinds of shapes with it. Look, you can even twist it around your finger. It makes a coil when I do that. Yes, it does look like a spring, doesn't it.

This is a wonderful box. Here's something that looks a lot like the wire. You can bend it and twist it. It must have wire inside of it, but the outside is fuzzy. It's really a ———. That's right, a pipe cleaner!

But let's see what else is in this box of surprises. Oh, here's something different! What could you do with this yarn that you couldn't do with the sticks or the wire? Of course, you can tie it. But it won't stay out straight like the sticks, and it won't stay twisted or bent the way the wire and the pipecleaner did.

Here's just a little piece of colored paper. I can't tie that, can I? And it won't stay bent or twisted. What can I do with this that I couldn't do with any of the other things? That's right, I can tear it! I can tear it into smaller pieces—or I can tear it into different shapes. You're right! I can also fold it.

I could do lots of different things with these wonderful surprises that came from my box. But there's one last thing way down in the bottom of the box. Here it is—a little piece of clay. I'll use that to hold all these other things together so that I can make a picture out of them.

See how the stick makes a tall straight line. I can tip it toward the side just a little bit—like that. Now let's see—I think I'll take that piece of wire and make a new shape out of it. I can bend it like this— or I can change it again and make it look like that. It looks good right here, so I'll push the end of it down into the clay.

Twist or bend the pipecleaner into an interesting shape and add it to your three-dimensional design. Then add the yarn and the paper—or whatever other materials you may have—until you have a completed design. Talk about letting the parts overlap and how the shapes change as you turn your "picture," not leaving any empty spaces.

Arrange some colored construction paper on a counter or empty table so that the children may display their work. You'll be surprised and delighted—and so will your class.

Make It Easy—for Yourself!

1. Have a variety of different types of materials: those that are rigid, that can be bent, twisted, tied, torn.

2. Give each child a small amount of non-hardening clay for the base. About a square inch of clay is fine.

3. Have a table or counter cleared where the arrangements may be displayed as they are finished.

4. Use familiar terms when talking about the design: make something important; fill the space. Turn the design as it is being made so that it looks complete (space filled) from all directions.

5. Give each child one of each type of material. Have extras available so that the children may choose from them whatever they need to complete their designs.

Variation

Use only applicator sticks (from medical supply) or toothpicks and non-hardening clay to create a three-dimensional design. Break the applicator sticks at various lengths. Use a small lump of clay to join the sticks. Keep the design small so that it doesn't become too heavy for the clay joints.

OBJECTIVES

1. **To introduce children to 3-D abstract designing.**

2. **To learn that shapes of various sizes make a more pleasing design.**

3. **To learn to create a design within a design—areas within areas.**

4. **To learn to use moving, "traveling" lines, that flow easily from one place to another to create a more sensitive design.**

(For grades 4 through 6, adapted to grades 2 and 3)

Lesson Five: Built-In Color!

TISSUE PAPIER MÂCHÉ

WOULDN'T IT BE WONDERFUL IF YOU COULD JUST make papier mâché that didn't look so dull and drab. Oh, of course you can always paint it to add color—but wouldn't it be nice if it had built-in color! Well, why not! Let's use colored tissue paper!

Tissue paper need not always be used as a transparent material or in an entirely two-dimensional way. Try it as a papier mâché to make interesting mobiles or to use as wall decorations.

Take a piece of tissue paper that has been cut to approximately 8 x 10 inches and hold it lengthwise in the air. Dip your fingers into

186

a soft, creamy wheat paste which has been distributed on a paper plate to each group of children. Then run your hand down the tissue paper, repeating this several times until a wet, string-like mass has developed from the flat, transparent paper.

Feel how soft and pliable the paper string has become. Lay it in a smooth flowing line on a piece of wax paper. Using another piece of tissue paper of the same color, repeat the process of forming into a wet string. Overlap onto the end of the first piece on the wax paper and continue to form the design. Add as many pieces as needed until the design is finished. A small loop may be made in the top as a part of the design so that later it will serve as a way of attaching a string.

Let the pieces cross over each other in several places to make more interesting sizes and shapes, and also to add strength and firmness to the finished design. As each string of tissue paper is added to the design, press it between the fingers into a smooth, slightly ridged line.

Place the wax paper and wet design where it can dry. It will not crack even if placed in the sun or directly over heat. When the tissue papier mâché is dry, the wax paper can be carefully pulled away, leaving a semi-three dimensional line design.

As each child finishes his design, have him wipe the excess paste from his hands with a paper towel, put it and any scrap of tissue paper (from the last piece, only!) on the paper plate, and put his wax paper with the design on it in a previously cleared space where it can dry. Have the last person to finish in each group take the paper plate with all the scraps on it and put it into the waste basket. Extra, unused tissue paper can be saved, and newspapers folded and thrown away. The clean-up is finished and the room is as clean and orderly as before.

When the tissue papier mâché has dried thoroughly and is hard, and the wax paper has been removed, the resulting designs will be flat on one side and ridged on the other side. If they are to be used as mobiles, attach a thin string or thread through the small loop or through the top of the design and suspend it as a mobile. They may be hung singly or in groups. They will make a more interesting display if allowed to hang at different lengths.

The one flat side also makes them excellent as wall decorations. Attach them flat against a bulletin board by bracing them with several straight pins placed at an angle to support them in various places. Intersperse them among other art exhibits, or use them to dress up a drab display of written papers. Let them slightly overlap the other displayed materials.

Make It Easy—for Yourself!

1. Cover all work surfaces with newspapers.
2. Mix wheat paste in a large can that can be discarded. (Perhaps a can from the school cafeteria.)
3. Distribute paste on paper plates that can be thrown away.
4. Have groups of three to six children working around one plate of paste—one color tissue paper for each group.
5. Use *every* scrap of tissue paper before getting another. (Even tiny pieces that pull off the wet "string" can be added to the design.)
6. Hold tissue paper over the work area, so that if any drops it will land on the newspaper.
7. Give each child a paper towel when materials are distributed. Place it under the wax paper until the design is finished. Then use it to wipe paste off hands until a thorough wash job can be done.

Variations

1. Use real things for motifs: birds, bugs, flowers, etc.
2. Use seasonal or holiday motifs.
3. Glue colored cellophane to some or all of the open areas.

Variations for Lower Grades

1. Use face tissue or paper napkins. Work directly on manila or construction paper. Do not remove design from paper. Use a brush to lightly color the top edge with tempera paint.
2. Use real things for motifs. Cut off excess background paper about one inch from edge of finished and dry picture.

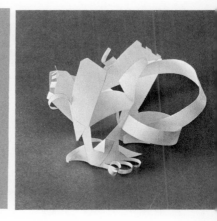

Lesson Six: Here a Cut, There a Cut

PAPER SCULPTURE

LET'S BE SCULPTORS TODAY! OH, NO, WE WON'T use wood, or stone, or plaster, or even clay. We'll just begin with a plain piece of white drawing paper. With a snip snip here and a twist twist there, here a cut, there a cut, everywhere a cut cut—and we have a piece of sculpture!

All you'll need will be a piece of 12 x 18 white drawing paper, a pair of scissors, and either paste or staplers. Now, let's see, what's the first thing we can do to change the shape of the paper? Cut it, of course! So here a cut and there a cut—long ones with easy, flowing lines, perhaps one down from the top and the other up from the side or bottom of the paper. Don't cut anything *off,* though—just make long cuts into the paper. Now what? We can take one long piece that has been cut and connect it with the

other piece that was cut. See, it makes a big loop with an open area
in between. Or we could connect each cut piece to a different place—
one fold coming toward us, the other fold away from us. That way
we have two open spaces. Either way will be a good beginning, so I'll
just attach them the way I think looks better. There, that makes the
paper three-dimensional already.

But why stop there! If one or two loops looks good, just think how
much better it can look. So make another cut or two into a large, plain
area. Find a good place to attach it so that it creates another open
space. Perhaps you can plan it so that it will show partly through one
of the other areas. Makes it more interesting, doesn't it!

But why stop there! Continue cutting into flat, plain areas and
rolling them back to meet some other part until the whole paper has
been transformed into a lovely, graceful, three-dimensional piece of
sculpture. Vary the sizes and shapes you create. Make the open areas
as important as—or even *more* important than—the solid areas. Turn
your piece of sculpture as you work on it so that it looks complete and
rhythmic from every angle. Notice how the shapes—solid *and* open
—appear to change as you turn your design! It can be startlingly
beautiful, especially if held in front of a piece of black paper. Make
a good mobile, wouldn't it!

But why stop there! Now that the lines you have cut sweep into
interesting, rhythmic shapes, let's dress them up a little more. Here's
a place where I could cut a narrow strip along the edge of the shape.
But this time I won't attach it to anything else. Instead, I'll make it
into a little curl, like a coil spring. I can run it along the open edge of
a pair of scissors or I can wrap it tightly around a pencil to make it
curl. See how it wiggles and moves as the mobile turns.

Find another place that needs some special decoration. Snip little
cuts in from the edge. Then bend one front, one back, front, back—
until all the edges have been folded, each in the opposite direction
from the one next to it. Fringe another spot to add extra interest.
Close the blades of a pair of scissors, and then carefully push them
through the paper in another area that looks too plain. Make some
tiny rounded holes; make others a little larger. Repeat some of these
same decorative effects.

There will be no scrap paper to collect as nothing has been cut off
the original 12 x 18 paper. Now, instead of being flat, it is a graceful,
three-dimensional piece of sculpture, in which the open areas are as
important as the paper itself. Hang them as mobiles from string of
varying lengths, so that they turn slightly to show what "here a cut,
there a cut" can really do!

Make It Easy—for Yourself!

1. Use 12 x 18 white drawing paper.
2. Emphasize the importance of using all the paper. None is to be discarded.
3. It is important to cut some lines well into the center of the paper, to avoid large flat areas on the completed three-dimensional design.
4. Curve back the cut pieces of paper in a wide variety of directions to create more interesting lines.
5. Use a variety of techniques to make the paper three-dimensional: cut and bend, curl, fold, pleat, twist, puncture.
6. If they are available, use tiny staplers instead of paste. With them, parts can be attached more quickly, making it possible to concentrate more completely on making the design.
7. If the tiny staplers are not available, give each child a small amount of paste on a piece of scrap paper.

Variations

1. Fold all of a piece of 12 x 18 white drawing paper into reverse pleats about an inch and a half wide. (Make the first fold about one and a half inches from the narrow edge. Fold that fold back on itself. Continue to do this all across the paper, each time reversing the direction of the fold.) Beginning on the first folded edge, cut a series of horizontal lines (a quarter to a half inch apart) that extend not quite to the next fold. Make the series of cuts continue from the top to the bottom of the fold. Then push through (in the opposite direction) every other cut section. Crease them as far back as they will go. This will result in a three-dimensional box-like design on this fold. On the next fold try another kind of cut: diagonal, curved, zig-zag. Whatever you start with, continue all the way down the fold. Reverse every other piece as you did on the first fold. Then try something different on the remaining folds. Be as original as you like!

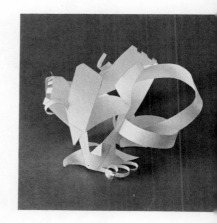

2. Experiment with many ways of making paper three-di-

mensional: make a paper curl (by rolling it around a pencil or running it along the edge of an open pair of scissors); cut out a simple oval shape, score it with a closed pair of scissors, bend it on the scored line; twist a thin piece of paper; fold a piece of paper into pleats. Arrange all of these experiments on a piece of black construction paper to create an interesting free-form, three-dimensional design.

3. Make a three-dimensional picture of something real. For example, make a three-dimensional face by curling paper for hair; scoring and bending paper for eyes, eyebrows, mouth; fringing and slightly curling paper for eyelashes. If all the parts are made from white paper, more emphasis can be placed on paper sculpture and the resulting light and shadow which it creates.

Variations for Lower Grades

1. Make a three-dimensional figure from strips of construction paper. Fasten the strips to form loops, and attach them to create any kind of object (person, animal, fish, flower, free-form). Hang them as mobiles.
2. Make any kind of picture from cut or torn construction paper. Make some part (or all of it) stand out from the background paper.

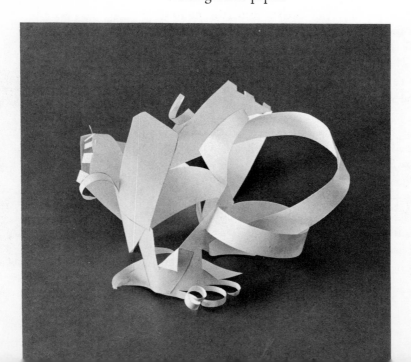

Lesson Seven: Pull It, Push It, Squeeze It!

NON-HARDENING CLAY

YOU CAN PULL IT, PUSH IT, SQUEEZE IT, ROLL IT— flatten it, break it, push a hole through it—pinch it, punch it, knead it, weld it, mold it—and even reuse it. What is it? *Clay*—imaginative, wonderful, clean, and exciting clay! We don't mean clay in its natural form, the kind you have to fire and glaze. We mean a non-hardening clay, science's adaptation of nature's own product, making it a more suitable and delightful medium for young children to enjoy.

Clay is wonderful to manipulate, but you can't squeeze it for an entire art period, so what do you do with it? The most logical answer is to make things; but what kind of things—and how? Children become frustrated and bored if they attempt to construct something too realistic and complicated beyond their realm of understanding and ability. For an introductory lesson in clay let's use an idea which is

193

MISCELLANEOUS

10

CHAPTER **10**

Miscellaneous Materials

Lesson One: Touch It!

COLLAGE

FROM GROCERY STORES TO GIFT SHOPS YOU SEE SIGNS that say, "Don't Touch," or "Please Don't Handle." You say the same thing. A thousand times you've said (and with good reason!), "Don't touch it!" But this time when we've finished our picture, we'll say, "Touch it!" Our collage will not only look good, but feel good, so—*touch it!*

Oh, this cotton batting feels so soft and fuzzy. So does this long piece of yarn. But not this scrap of metal! It is ———?

You're right! It is hard. Things don't all feel the same, do they? What can you touch that feels soft? What can you feel that is hard?

Without even having to get up and move about, each child will be able to discover something nearby that is soft—perhaps a soft sweater, or even the side of his face. Then find something that is hard—the top of his desk, the glasses he is wearing. Don't forget to find something rough *and* something smooth. It's surprising how many textures are within your reach. Just—touch it!

When you have investigated the feel of several different textures that are nearby—and several that you have gathered together for this purpose—pass out cards on which you have written the name of a texture. Make it a game. Don't let anyone else see your card—keep your texture a secret. Some of you will be lucky to have "Rough" on your card. Then you can use this wonderful corrugated paper—or the sandpaper. That would be *really* rough. Or if your card says "Soft," how good that cotton batting or angora yarn will feel. There are so many soft things you can choose from. But, then, if you have "Smooth" or "Hard" there are so many things to choose from, too, aren't there? That shiny piece of metal is both hard and smooth, isn't it? So you could use it for either of those textures. Get those cards out of sight so that no one but you knows what it says. Later we'll— touch it!

After everyone has been assigned a texture in this way, let groups of children choose several items that are rough, or smooth, or hard, or soft—depending upon what is written on their card. A piece of 12 x 18 construction paper for the background, and each child is ready to begin his collage—a design of overlapping materials.

Be careful what color you choose for your background. You know some colors look soft while others make you think of hard, rough, or smooth. Pink or light blue looks softer than bright red or dark blue, doesn't it?

Encourage the class to begin with the larger areas of their collage. Small things can be added later, perhaps right on top of some of the bigger things. Return extra materials to the supply area and choose whatever other items are needed to complete the collage. Move parts from place to place to find the spot on the collage that is just right for them. Then paste, glue, or even sew them (depending on the material) to the background.

Last of all, stand back and admire them. You'll be surprised how interesting a texture collage can be. There won't be any doubt about whether it is soft, or hard, or rough, or smooth. But, oh yes, be sure to——touch it!

Make It Easy—for Yourself!

1. Have a wide assortment of materials of various textures. Some that are easily obtainable are:
   Soft: cotton batting, flannel, yarn, cotton roving, sponge rubber, gum eraser, felt.
   Hard: tongue depressors, wire, wood, shells, scrap metal.
   Rough: corrugated cardboard, crumpled tissue paper (or aluminum foil), broken tongue depressors, twigs, sandpaper, bits of dry sponge, coarse string, wire screening.
   Smooth: aluminum foil, smooth cloth, sandpapered wood, plastic, shiny paper, scrap metal.
   Spread them out on a table or counter so that children may choose what they need.
2. Have both paste and glue available. Paste is easier to use with paper or cloth, but will not hold such things as wood or shells. A stapler would be handy to have to attach wire or twigs.
3. Work large—12 x 18 paper for the background is a good size.
4. Begin collage with materials that form a large mass (cloth, paper, foil), then add the line materials (yarn, wire, twigs) and the tiny items. This builds up a background on which the smaller items may be placed.
5. Allow children to get more materials or return extras as the case may be.
6. No pencils! Let the materials create their own patterns without any preliminary drawing.

Variations

1. Create *color* collage rather than *texture* collage. Work with many variations of a single color. Cover all of the background for this type of collage. Variety of texture will help to increase color variety and give added interest if you want to combine both elements of art.

2. Begin with a specific theme: dance music, basketball, skating, stamp collecting. Try to interpret the theme in a collage without making a realistic picture.

Variations for Lower Grades

1. Use all types of textures on a single collage.
2. Find a variety of papers which look (rather than feel) as though they are textured. Paste them together to create a collage.

Lesson Two: Has to Be Fun!

CRUMPLED TISSUE PAPER FLOWERS

SPRINGTIME, FLOWERS, GAY TISSUE PAPER—AND an art lesson that combines them all just *has* to be fun! Make flowers that are big, that are partly three-dimensional—and you'll beam with pride when they're finished.

Talk for a few minutes about flowers—not roses, or zinnias, or pansies, or any other real flower—just *flowers,* the most beautiful ones you could ever see. What would the blossom look like? Would the petals be pointed or rounded? Would it be one color or more than one color? Would all the petals be one size or different sizes? Get the children thinking and seeing, each in his own way.

Then begin with a piece of 12 x 18 manila or white drawing paper. Let each child draw in the outline of a big blossom. Urge them to make it big—the blossom is the beautiful part of the flower. Don't

202

bother with small parts or with the stem or leaves. They will come later. Use white chalk for the drawing to encourage making the shapes big and so that the drawing will not show when the flower is finished.

Inside one large petal, "paint" on a layer of paste. Crumple a small piece of tissue paper, and, after having opened it slightly again, lay it onto the pasted area and lightly press it down. Shape the petal by pushing the tissue paper to the edges of the pasted area. Because the tissue paper was crumpled, it will lay in a rough, three-dimensional mass.

Continue painting on an area of paste and filling it with the wrinkled tissue paper. When the blossom is nearly finished, encourage each child to stop work, hold his paper at arm's length, and look at it carefully and critically. What can be done to make it even more beautiful? Does it look too small on the paper? If so, perhaps you can think of some way of making it bigger—adding on another larger shape around the edge or extending out some of the smaller parts. Or does it look too plain? Perhaps you could add some smaller parts inside the design using another color or another shade of the same color. Then, go back to work and continue until all of the blossom is finished.

Stem and leaves come last of all. Finish them with the same technique as the blossom, or use construction paper. If construction paper is used, cut a stem slightly longer than the area on which it will be pasted. Then put just a little paste on each end of the stem, push one and well up under the crumpled tissue paper flower and attach the other end to the paper so that the rest of the stem—the center part—rounds up off the paper rather than laying flat. It will create a little "tunnel" under the stem. Cut the leaves and paste on flat or put on just a spot of paste at the bottom and so that the rest of the leaf will remain free from the paper.

As a final touch, show the class how they can trim off the corners of the white paper so as to make a more interesting background shape. Use the general shape of the blossom, stem, and leaves to cut out a big free-form shape around them. Then, make an interesting display, sit back and admire them, and wait for compliments.

Make It Easy—for Yourself!

1. Use the paper cutter to cut tissue paper into small pieces, about 4 x 5 inches.

2. Place an assortment of colored tissue paper in several parts of the room so that only a few children will be going to any one place to get supplies.

3. Collect the chalk soon after the initial sketch has been made. This prevents drawing extra tiny, fussy parts, and avoids the possibility of the chalk getting on the floor to be stepped on, creating unnecessary problems.

4. Keep fingers out of the paste. Sticky fingers and tissue paper are a poor combination. Use paste brushes—or use an applicator made by folding a piece of scrap paper several times.

5. Give each child a small amount of paste on a piece of scrap paper.

Variations

1. Use in combination with colored construction paper, either adding some of the details with construction paper or beginning with a construction paper base and adding crumpled tissue paper parts to it.

2. Use other motifs: animals, birds, fish, people.

Variation for Grades K through 2

Use other pliable papers: paper napkins, face tissue, paper towels. Put the paste on in an outline. Crumple the paper and lay it on top of the pasted line. Touch the top edge of the crumpled paper with tempera paint—just enough to add a bit of color.

Variation for Grades 5 and 6

Use as a mural. Make all the individual parts with this technique. Then either paste or tack them to the background.

OBJECTIVES

1. To realize that dye can be used in other than the conventional ways.

2. To see the possibilities for combining unusual materials in order to create a new technique.

3. To blend colors in order to achieve more pleasing varieties.

(For grades 5 and 6)

Lesson Three: Let's Draw with Tape

DYE

PERHAPS YOU'VE TRIED THE USUAL—OR EVEN SOME of the more unusual—techniques with dye. Or perhaps you've been a little bit afraid and stayed as far away from it as possible. In either case, let's try something simple but quite out of the ordinary.

We'll paint a picture with *dye*. Of course that calls for cloth, so we'll use unbleached muslin torn into pieces from about 9 x 12 to almost 12 x 18. A few other materials will be needed, too, but those come later. First of all, what will you paint?

Why, you can paint anything that ordinarily you would put on a piece of paper. It may be a still life, a landscape, a seascape, a portrait —anything you feel in the mood for at the moment.

First we'll "draw" the picture with pieces of masking tape. Tape is ideal because it can be cut into narrow strips and adhered to the cloth in lines that stop the flow of dye. When the tape is removed later it results in an outline—or drawing—of each part of the picture. Or, it can be put on in larger areas to form white silhouettes that are an important part of the picture when the tape is removed. In this way part of the picture can be "painted" with tape. Be sure to have the tape flat against the cloth so that there aren't any openings where the dye can flow under it.

Now that you've drawn your picture with tape, the next step is to paint on the dye. Regular watercolor brushes work fine for that. And remember that dye can be mixed—just as can paint—to blend new color varieties. Painting on cloth is a little bit different from painting on paper. Of course, the cloth absorbs the dye faster than paper absorbs paint, so you'll need to use much more dye. You'll want to mix the dye before you put it on the cloth, too, so that it will go on more evenly. But see how easy it is. The tape is just like a fence that stops the color. Oh, be careful not to use so much dye that it goes right over the top of that tape line. There—that didn't take long. The painting is all finished.

When the dye has dried enough to permit handling the "painting," the most exciting part of the whole process begins—removing the tape. As each piece is pulled off, a clean, sharp edge—almost stencil-like—appears. The removal of each piece of tape is a happy surprise. It was *fun*—and a rewarding experience—to draw with tape and paint with dye.

Make It Easy—for Yourself!

1. Emphasize the property of dye that makes it different from paint. It is a color meant to be permanent—not to wash out. This is an advantage, but can create problems unless it is understood and precautions taken.
2. Wear old clothes and have them completely covered with an old shirt worn backwards to button in the back. This is good "insurance."
3. Keep the supply of dye in one area that is thoroughly covered with newspaper. Permit only a limited number of children to be in that area at any one time.
4. Fasten the muslin to a slightly larger piece of manila or

construction paper. A piece of tape on two sides will do fine. This keeps the cloth stretched evenly, making a better work surface, and also provides a protective area when the dye is applied.

5. Give each child a long strip of masking tape (nearly a yard long). Fasten it to the edge of the desk and let it hang down the side. This enables each child to have a reasonable supply at hand without it becoming matted together.

6. Take plenty of time "drawing" with the tape. This is the longest part of the lesson and may not all be finished in one art lesson. Painting on the dye is done quickly.

7. Have each child blend each color of his dye in a tiny jar. Small pill bottles would be fine. Finish painting all the areas to be done with any one color dye before going on to another color.

8. Concentrated liquid batik dye (water must be added to the concentrate) comes easy to use, but any type of dye can be mixed to form a liquid—then blended with other colors by the children to form their own varieties.

9. An easy way to dispense the dye is to put a milk straw in each container of dye. Place a finger over the opening of the straw to lift out a small quantity of dye and transfer it to individual bottles for blending. Add water to thin the dye to the desired shade.

Variations

1. Use half or three-quarter inch wide masking tape to create a Mondrian-type design. The design will be made up entirely of vertical and horizontal lines to create a pleasing arrangement of shapes. Use from one to three varieties of dye to "paint" the design. Remove the tape.

2. Use white wax crayon in place of the tape. The wax in the crayon will resist the dye just as it does paint. When the dye is dry, press the cloth with a warm iron to remove the wax from the crayon. (Cover the cloth with newspaper before pressing to prevent smudging.) Or, plain white wax candles may be used in place of white crayons. Then all the wax is pressed out without leaving white lines.

3. Fold the material being used into any kind of a fold. You

can use an accordion fold, napkin fold, or invent your own. When the folding is done, simply dip part of the fabric in different colors of dye, rotating the folded material until every outside corner is colored. When the fabric is opened, an unusual and striking pattern is discovered. If the primary colors are used and they bleed together, a startling change of colors will occur.

Lesson Four: Hold That Line!

JERSEY LOOPS AND COTTON ROVING

A CRAYON CAN MAKE A LINE—SO CAN A PIECE OF chalk or even a paintbrush. But somethings are *already* lines—like these jersey loops, or yarn, or roving. Just put them where you want them, then—hold that line! A bit of paste will do that for you.

Have a big box of various colors of jersey loops, bits of cotton roving, short pieces of yarn. Scraps will do just as well as fresh supplies. Mix them all together, and every time you reach in and bring out a handful there will be a variety of materials as well as a variety of colors.

Show the class what you have. Pull out a handful of scraps and let them drop slowly from your hand. Repeat the motions several times. Scraps—but interesting scraps, aren't they? I wonder what you could do with them. Look at all the colors—see how thick and fat some pieces are, and how thin some of the yarn is.

209

Oh, here's something different! Look, the jersey loop has begun to come apart—ravel, that is. See how fine each little strand is and how curly they all are. The jersey loop doesn't look at all the same when it is raveled, does it. Could you change anything else to look different? Certainly, you could separate the strands of the cotton roving—and maybe the yarn, too. Yes, you would just pull it apart so that it looks fuzzy. Looks almost like colored cotton batting, doesn't it?

Try to get your class thinking about ways of changing the appearance of the original materials. The more variety you get—and the more thinking the children do—the more varied and interesting will be the finished pictures. Ask what the raveled jersey loops remind them of—what could they become in a picture? What could you do with the fuzzy yarn or cotton roving?

Well, you have lots of ideas so let's put them into a picture—any kind of a picture. A picture with mountains in it that you thought the raveled jersey loops would be good for—or a funny clown with fuzzy hair—or just patterns of shapes and lines. Choose the materials and the colors you want. Change the way the materials look, if you like. Perhaps you can even think of some other ways of changing and using them. Plan your own picture. Make it just as different as you can.

Colored or white paper, a handful of scrap materials, a little bit of paste and lots of imagination will combine to produce some of the most intriguing pictures you've seen in a long time. As the children work on their pictures have them think of an original title—not just any old title, but one which captures the mood as well as the appearance of the picture. Display the pictures and titles together.

Make It Easy—for Yourself!

1. Have a variety of weaving and stitchery materials—cotton roving, jersey loops, yarn—in a wide range of colors. Scrap materials are as good as new ones for this lesson.
2. Give each child or group of children a handful of whatever materials are available. Encourage them to use those which they have, but permit exchanges with other children.
3. No pencils! Let the materials form their own lines and shapes.

4. Encourage children to use the materials in a variety of ways: the materials just as they are to form lines in their pictures; massed together to form shapes; jersey loops raveled; yarn or roving separated into strands, or pulled apart to be fuzzy.
5. Have 12 x 18 white drawing paper and several colors of construction paper so that children may choose the color they want for a background.
6. Distribute paste on small pieces of scrap paper.
7. Have each child write his title on the back of his picture so that you may display title and picture together. Don't spoil the picture by having any words on it.

Variations

1. Use cotton roving, yarn, or jersey loops to create a line drawing of a big object. Complete the picture with other media (crayons, paint, chalk, paper).
2. Use any one or a combination of these linear materials to create a non-objective picture. Break up the space on a 12 x 18 paper into pleasing shapes and sizes. Unify the design by repeating some of the shapes. Overlap and group to form an interesting picture.
3. Use any scrap materials in a similar way. For example, save all the scraps of colored paper left from a cut paper lesson. Give each person a handful of scraps picked at random from a box. Have each child use *all* the scraps he receives to create an abstract or non-objective picture. ("Of course, you may cover up some of the scraps if you don't want them to show—but nothing left over!")

Lesson Five: Breakthrough!

PRINT-MAKING

A BREAKTHROUGH IN SCIENCE OR SPACE TRAVEL IS always a moment of great excitement. In fact, a discovery in any field is exciting. In the art world a major breakthrough has been found in the field of print-making in the classroom. This valuable and creative art form has been neglected in the primary grades because of its seeming difficulty and the apparent need for using specialized tools. The breakthrough has come about with the adaptation of printing techniques to simple materials and basic skills.

We offer you an easy, effective way of making beautiful prints. All you need is thin oaktag, scissors, paper, paste, and printing supplies (roller and ink). In order to make a print you must have a raised surface, so we'll take our oaktag and create a composition by cutting out parts of it and pasting them onto our 9 x 12 manila paper. In this way we create a composition which may be either realistic or abstract.

You may want to cut out an animal, a face, a flower, a boat, or even a telescope on a tripod. Perhaps you would prefer making a design of geometric or free-form shapes. You can make almost anything, but keep the basic shapes and designs simple. You can overlap pieces, too. For example, a face may be made by cutting out a head shape. Then eyes, nose, and a mouth may be cut and overlapped onto the oval head. These areas are built up higher, and will show up, therefore, in the final printing.

When the cardboard picture is finished, ink must be applied. This built-up picture then becomes our printing plate. Spread a small amount of water-soluable printing ink on a glass plate or metal pan. Take the brayer (roller) and roll it across the ink, spreading it out on the glass. Continue to roll the brayer over the ink until the brayer is uniformly covered with ink. Then roll the brayer on the plate (the cardboard picture) until all of the raised areas are covered. Some ink will go onto the manila paper. This will improve the print by adding interesting background texture.

Take a piece of 9 x 12 white or light colored construction paper and place it over the inked plate. Firmly, with the soft part of your fist, rub the paper over the inked plate. Carefully pull off the top sheet, and *presto!*—you have a professional-looking print. Many copies may be made from this one plate by reinking and pressing for each new print. This simple procedure was really a breakthrough in the ancient art of print-making.

Make It Easy—for Yourself!

1. Cover desks with newspaper.
2. Set up four or five printing stations. One at the end of each row of seats is a good arrangement. Place a brayer, glass, and ink at each station.
3. Have the students complete their cutting and pasting at their seats, cleaning up all scraps and paste before doing any printing.
4. Have each student select his white or colored paper and leave it at his desk. Only the plate should be brought to the printing station.
5. After inking the plate, it should be carried back to the student's desk. The actual print-making is done at that time.

6. Water soluable inks are easily washed off the glass or metal pans and rollers.

Variations

1. Use a thick cardboard to create the plate. This will cause sharper definition of cutout objects.
2. Use toothpicks for the plate to make a linear picture.
3. Use cork for part of the plate to produce a print of many textures.
4. Use heavy cord or cotton roving glued to the plate to make a graceful linear composition.
5. Cut tiny slots around the edge of a cardboard rectangle. Use string to create a straight line design on the cardboard. The slots will hold the string in place.

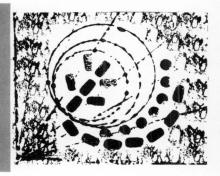

OBJECTIVES

1. To introduce a simple form of printing to young children.

2. To see the possibilities of using ordinary materials as a means of creating art.

3. To develop a sense of rhythm through repetition.

(For grades 3 through 6, adapted to grades 1 and 2)

Lesson Six: Gadgets, Gadgets, and More Gadgets!

REPEAT PRINTING

WE'RE ALL GADGET HAPPY! JUST GIVE US A NEW gadget—from a bulldozer to a new style can opener— and we're so enthusiastic we're practically new people. We're curious to see how it works and what we can do with it. So let's make use of that creative imagination in an art lesson that has gadgets, and gadgets, and more gadgets!

Our gadgets will be of the simplest kind. We're going to print them, so make sure there is some easy way of holding on to them. For example, an ordinary paper clip is too thin and lies too flat against a paper to be able to handle it for printing. Of course, you could print the side or one end of it. But how can you print it to look like the curved shape of a paper clip? Why, just bend upward one end of the wire—to have something to hold on to. Other simple

215

gadgets won't require any changing—bottle cork, screw top to a jar, thin edge of a tongue depressor, flat side of an eraser, empty spool for thread, either end of a paper cup.

Now what can we do with these gadgets? Print with them—wonderful repeat patterns, wild abstracts, or realistic pictures. You'll need paint—one color tempera paint, or as many colors as you think will look good. Brush a small amount of paint onto the edge of the gadget to be printed. Press the painted surface on the paper you are printing (white drawing paper or colored construction paper), and there is a reproduction of the shape of the gadget you printed! Let's try it again. Repaint the edge to be printed, press it against the paper—and another print just like the first one. Print it again and again, using only one gadget, or try a different one—one that's a different shape or a different size.

The rounding line of a jar top creates a graceful curve. The long edge of a tongue depressor gives you a strong, straight line. Use your imagination in finding gadgets as well as using them. What kind of a print would a fork make? Or a potato masher? Or try the ends of erasers, or the rim of an oblong box—or ——the list is endless!

You'll have lots of fun trying out different prints and the patterns you can make with them. The important thing is to have a wide variety of gadgets, and gadgets, and more gadgets!

Make It Easy—for Yourself!

1. Have enough simple gadgets available so that each child will be able to use several.
2. Cover all work areas with newspaper.
3. Use very little paint on a gadget. Too much paint tends to blot.
4. Sometimes the first printing of an object—especially a metal one—is not satisfactory. Therefore have a piece of scrap paper for each child to print on once before putting it on his picture.
5. A few drops of tempera paint on a piece of scrap paper makes a satisfactory palette. At the end of the lesson the palette paper can be folded inside the newspaper and thrown away.
6. A paste brush makes a good tool for applying paint to the gadget—better than a soft watercolor brush.

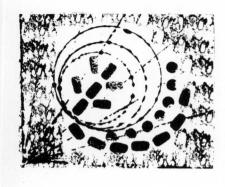

Variation

Cut a potato or a carrot in half and print with that. Or make simple cuts into the flat surface of the potato or carrot and print it.

Variations for Lower Grades

1. Use only paper cups and tongue depressors to print with. This will give both curved and straight lines. Make realistic or non-objective pictures.
2. Use a small rectangular piece of thin cardboard as the printing tool. Use it straight or bend it into various kinds of lines before printing with it.

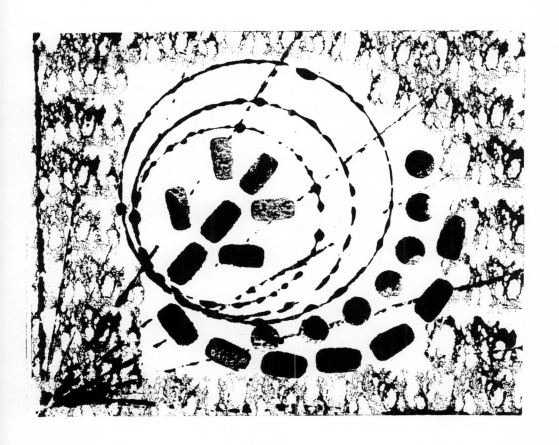

Index

Date Due

OCT 2 '69		
JA 29 '71		
FAC		
FAC		
FACULTY		
DE 7 '73		
fac